AERONAUTICAL ENGINEERING DIPLOMA & ENGINEERING MCQ

MANOJ DOLE

Made with ♥ on the Notion Press Platform
www.notionpress.com

Contents

Foreword

Aeronautical Engineering Diploma & Engineering MCQ is a simple Book for Aeronautical Diploma & Engineering Course, Revised Syllabus, It contains objective questions with underlined & bold correct answers MCQ covering all topics including all about the latest & Important about Applied Science, Basic Electrical and Electronics Engineering, Computer Aided Engineering Drawing, Elements of Aeronautics, Engineering Drawing, Engineering Mathematics, Fluid Mechanics and Pneumatics, Aircraft Instrumentation System, Aircraft Jet Engine, Aircraft Manufacturing Technology, Aircraft Materials, Aircraft Piston Engineering, Aircraft Electrical System, Avionics and Aircraft Radio System, Basic Aerodynamics, Basic Aircraft Structure and SOM, Helicopter Basics, Maintenance Management, Professional Ethics and Indian Constitution, Thermodynamics for Aeronautical Engineering, Aircraft Inspection, Maintenance and Repair, Civil Aircraft Regulations, Civil Aviation Regulation(CAR), Flight Safety, Organisational Management, Rocket and Satellites, General Subjects, Applied Mathematics, Applied Science, Basic Electrical and Electronics Engineering and lots more.

We add new question answers with each new version. Please email us in case of any errors/omissions. This is arguably the largest and best e-Book for All engineering multiple choice questions and answers.

As a student you can use it for your exam prep. This e-Book is also useful for professors to refresh material.

Preface

This book may be purchased for educational, business, or sales promotional use. Online edition is also available for this title. For more information, contact our corporate/institutional sales department: [+919921582799] or [manojdole1@gmail.com]

While every precaution has been taken in the preparation of this book, the publisher and authors assume no responsibility for errors or omissions, or for damages resulting from the use of the information contained herein.

About the Author

MANOJ DOLE is an Engineer from reputed University. He is currently working with Government Industrial Training- Institute as a lecturer from last 12 Years. His interest include- Engineering Training Material, Invention & Engineering Practical- Knowledge etc.

CHAPTER ONE

Aeronautical Engineering Hand Tools & Measuring Instrument Theory

Download App
Online Test Exam
ITI Books
AutoCAD CAM
JOB & Apprentice
Online Theory
Computer Course
Trading Course
CNC Course
MSCIT Course
Shopping Business
Internet Business
Web Designing
Online Services
Top Sportsmans
Indian Army
Freedom Fighters
Top Scientists
Social Reformers
Motivational Speaker
Top Richest People
Join WhatsApp Group
Join Facebook Group
Like Facebook Page
PAN / Adhar / Licence Passport

Fire extinguisher

Calliper

Hacksaw frame

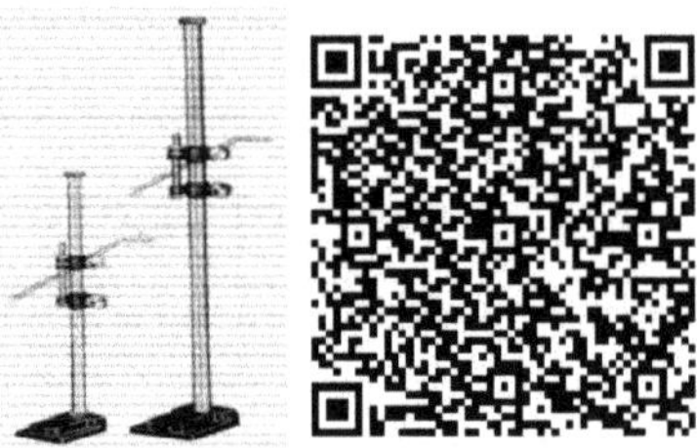

Universal surface guage

Hammer

Centre punch

Bench vice

Files

Scraper

Surface Plate

Outside Micrometer

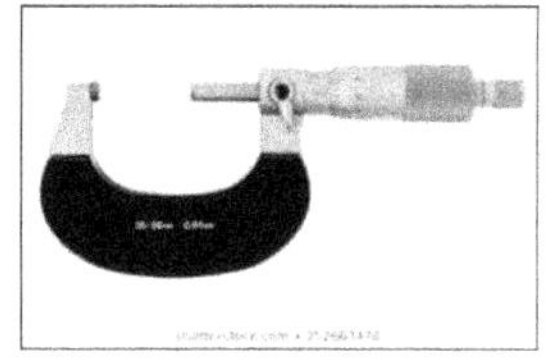

Micrometer

Depth micrometer

Vernier Calliper

Vernier bevel protractor

Drilling

Reamer

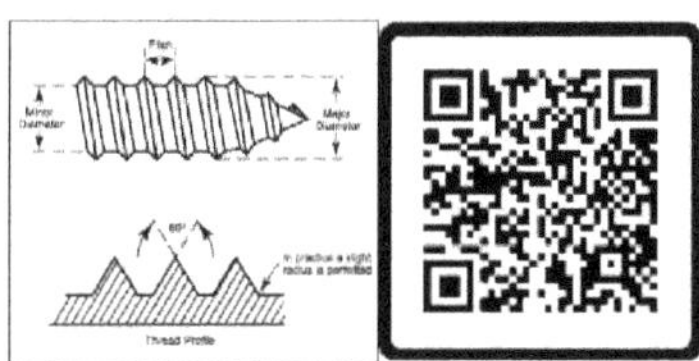

Thread

Tap Die

Grinding Wheel

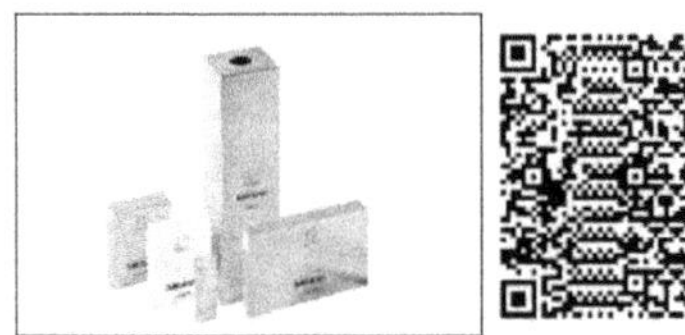

Slip gauge

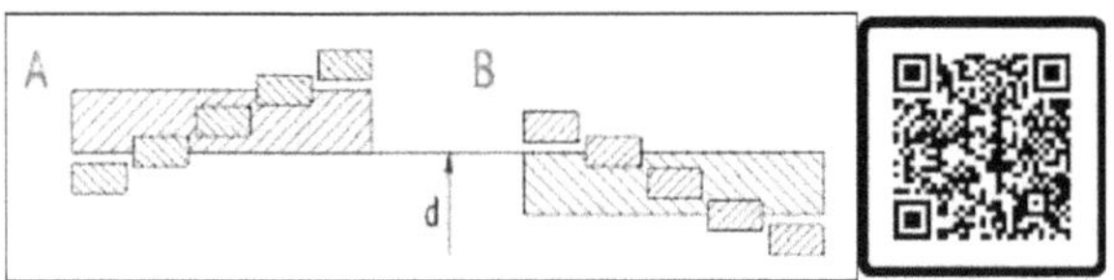

Limit fit tolerance

Lathe Machine

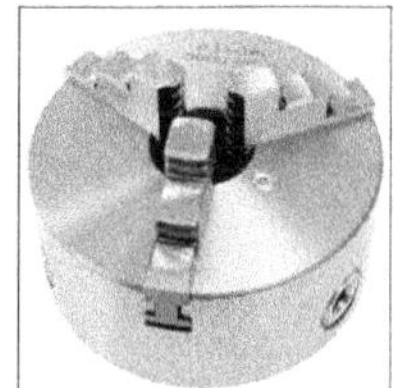

Lathe chuck

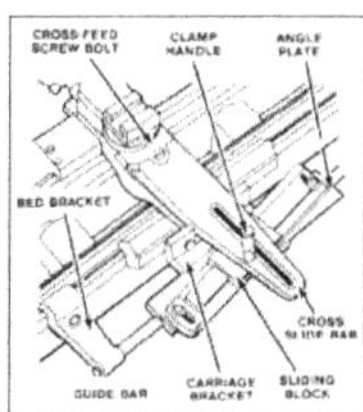

Taper turning attachment

taper ring gauge

screw pitch gauge

Gear

screw pitch gauge

Tap Die

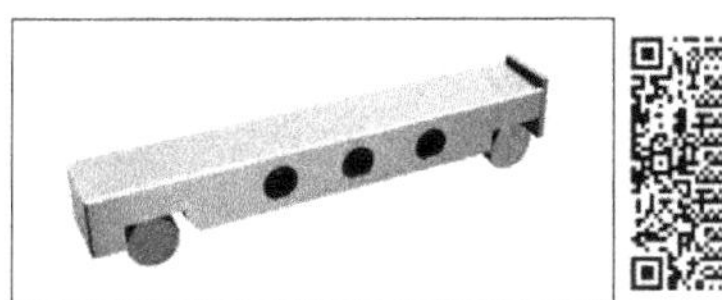

Sine bar

Slip gauge

Dial test indicator

Telescopic gauge

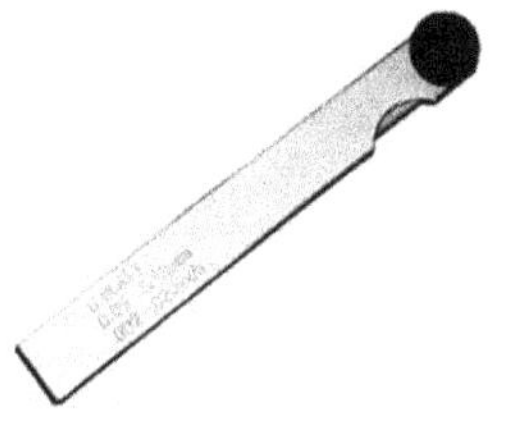 

Feeler gauge

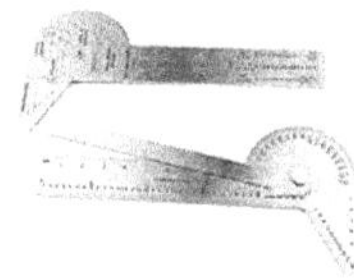 

Centre gauge

Jig

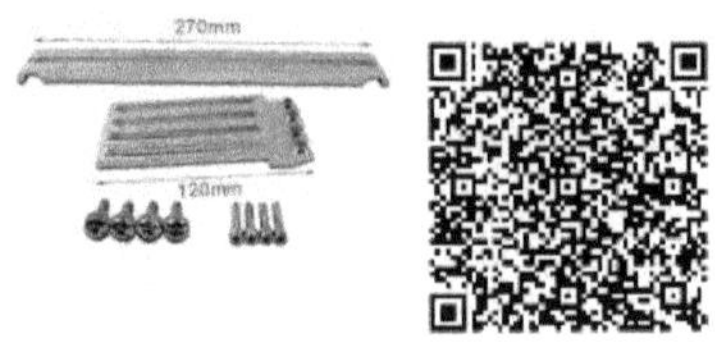

Fixture

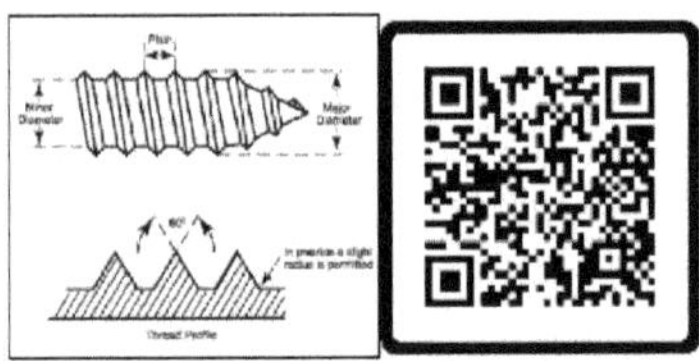

Thread

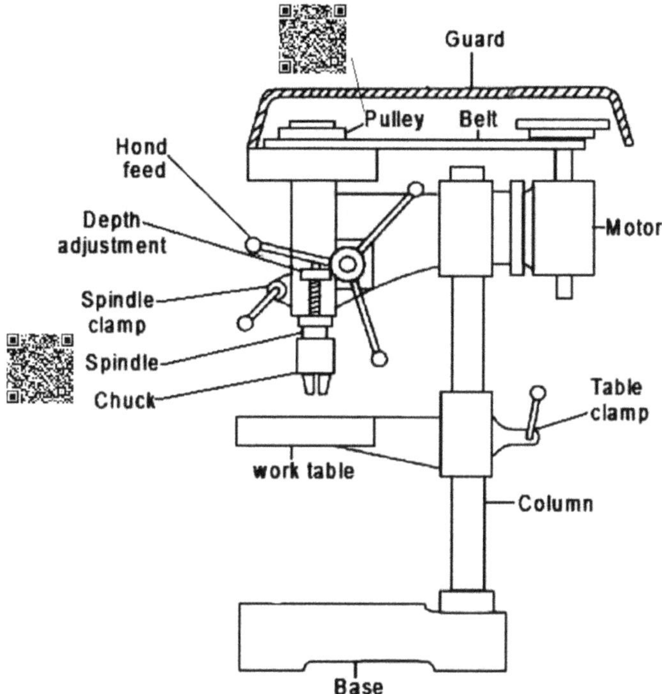

Piller Drilling Machine

CHAPTER TWO

Aeronautical Engineering Drawing Theory

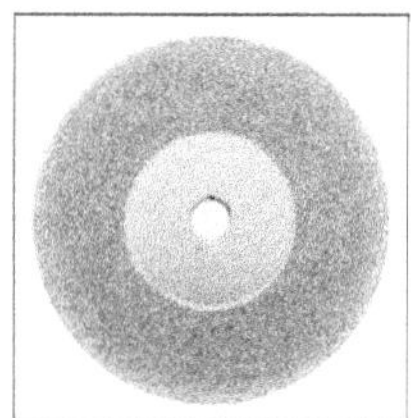

Grinding

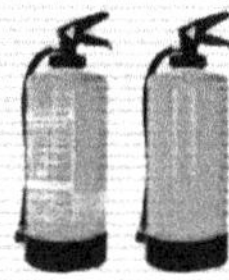

Fire extinguisher

French curve in drawing

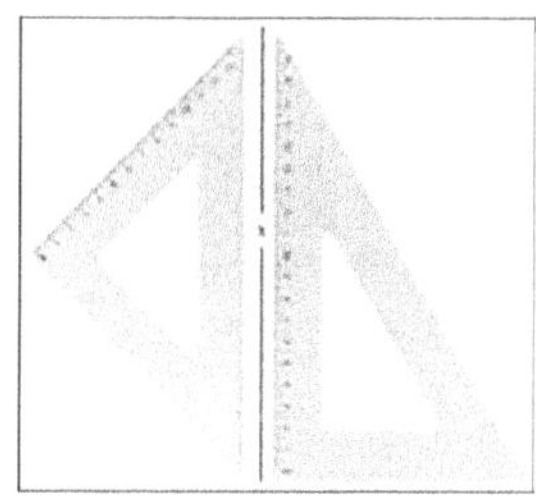

Set square in drawing

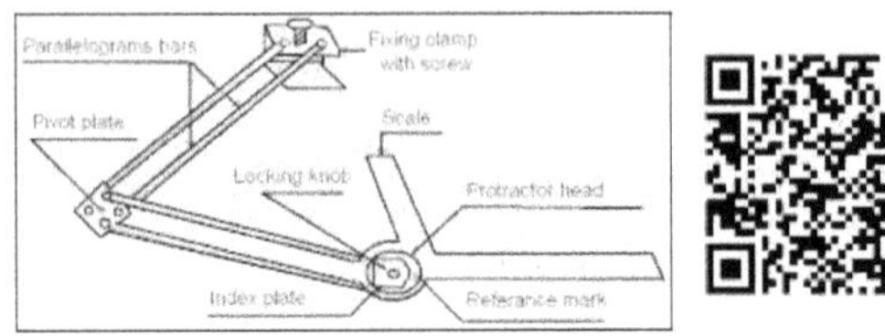

Mini drafter in drawing

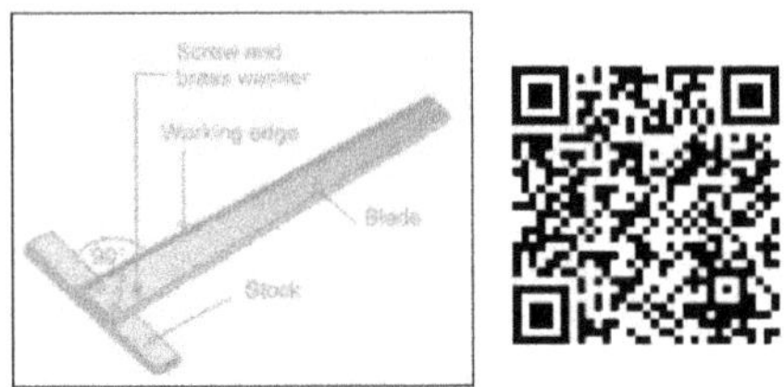

T - square in drawing

Cams in engine

Orthographic projection in drawing

Third angle projection drawing

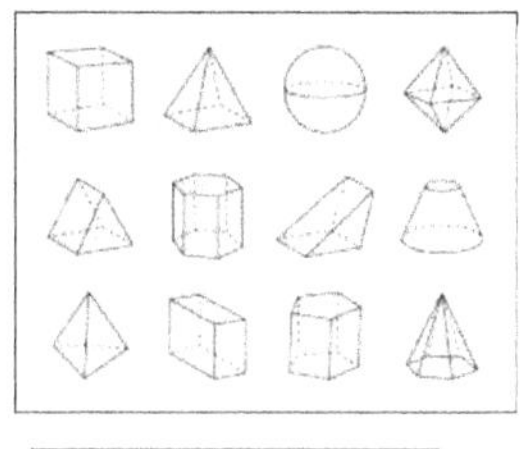

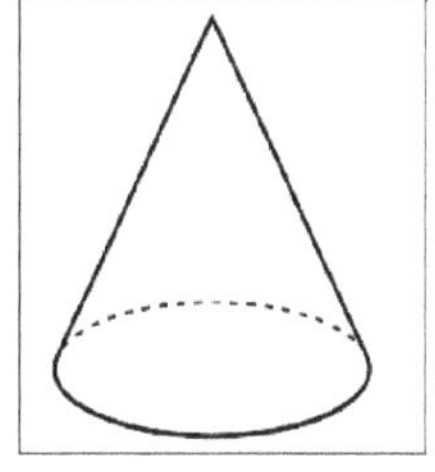

Cone in engineering drawing

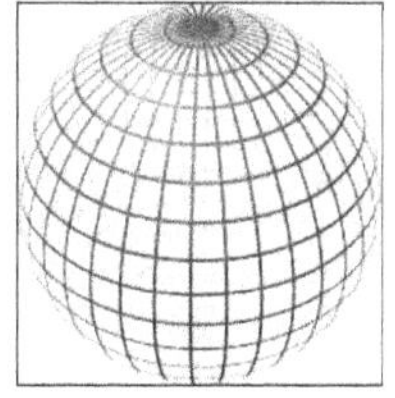

Sphere in drawing

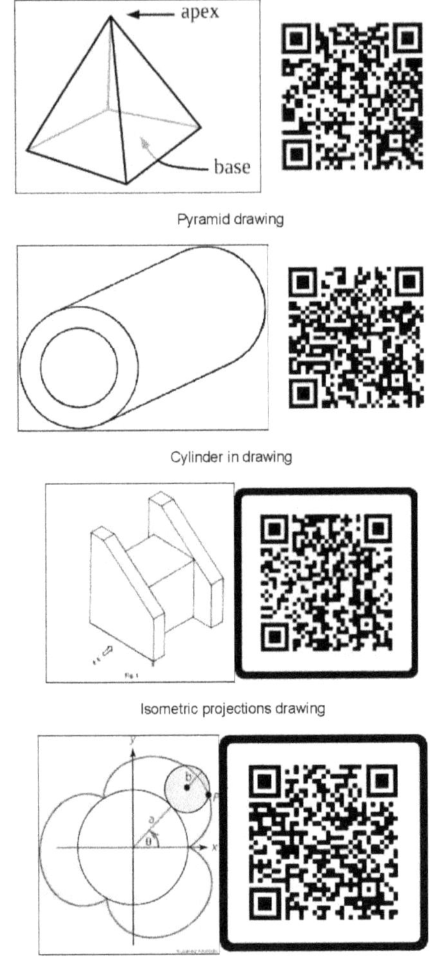
apex
base
Pyramid drawing
Cylinder in drawing
Isometric projections drawing
y
b
P
a
θ
x
Curves engineering drawing

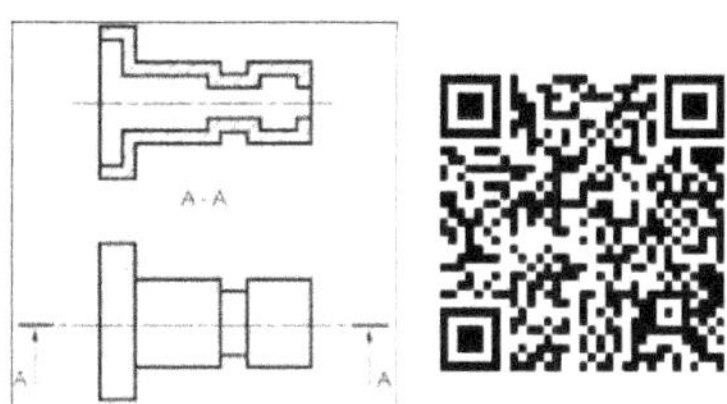

Sectional views in drawing

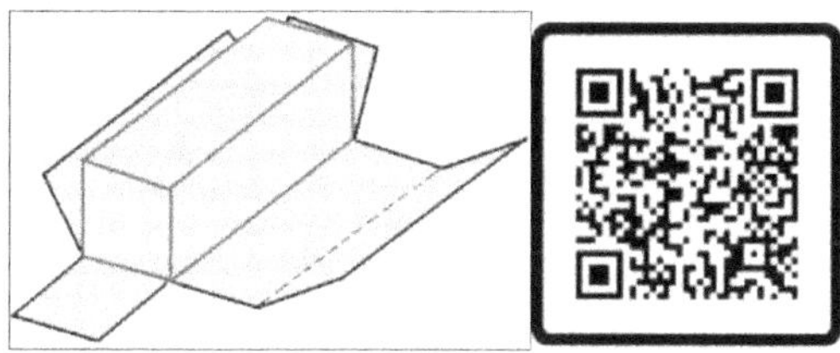

Development of surfaces in drawing

Hexagonal plane in drawing

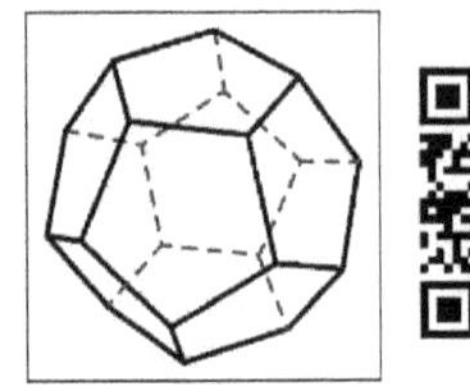

Polyhedron in drawing

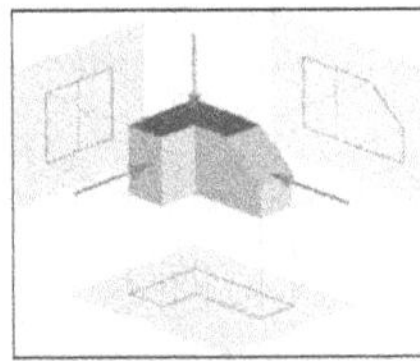

First Angle projection method in drawing

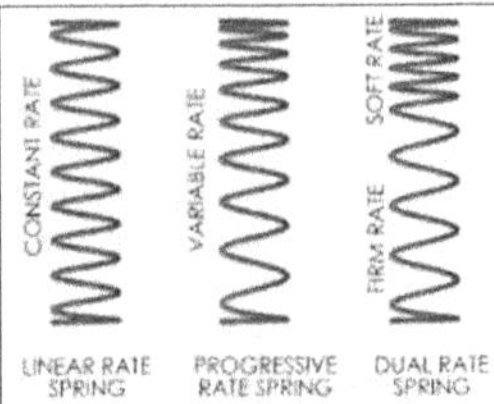

Springs in drawing

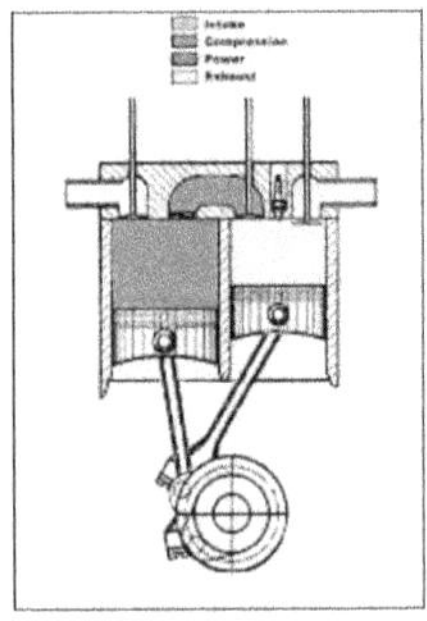

Engine in vehicle

CHAPTER THREE

Aeronautical Engineering Electrical Theory

14 ITI Book MCQ - Manoj Dole
www.itibook.com
battery
capacitor
cell
dynamometer
electromagnet
heater
inductance
magnet
www.itigov.blogspot.com www.jobapprentices.blogspot.com www.ititests.blogspot.com
www.itibook.com

15 ITI Book MCQ - Manoj Dole
www.itibook.com
megger
motor
multimeter
ohmmeter
resistores
star connected alternator
voltmeter ammeter
wattmeter
www.itigov.blogspot.com www.jobapprentices.blogspot.com www.ititests.blogspot.com
www.itibook.com

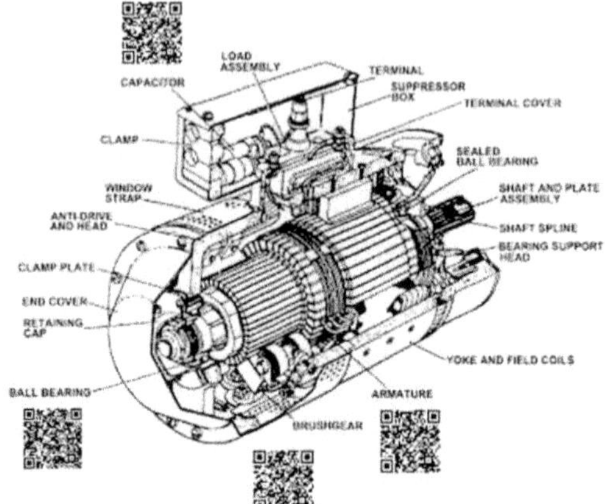

Electrical Generator

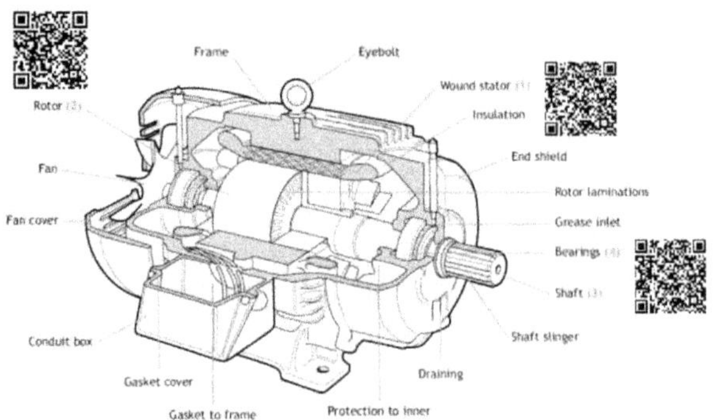

Electrical Induction Motor

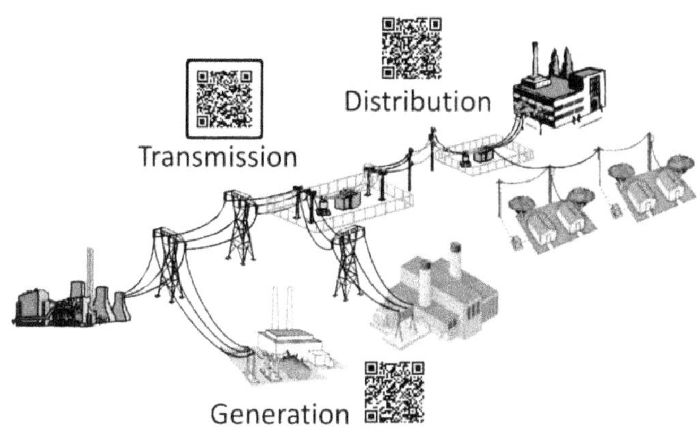

Electrical Power Distribution

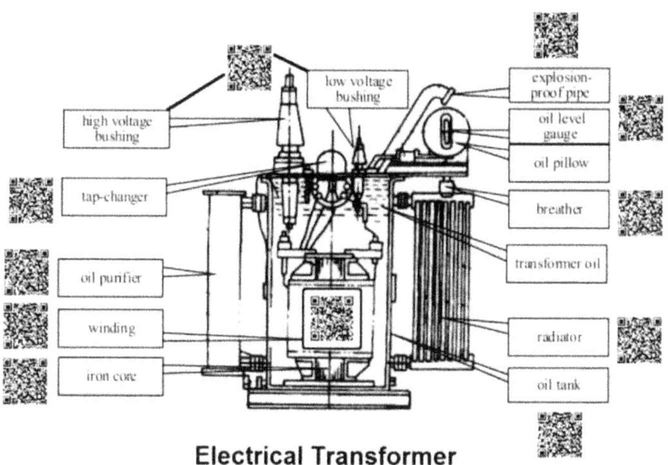

Electrical Transformer

CHAPTER FOUR

Aeronautical Engineering Hydraulics & Pnumatics Theory

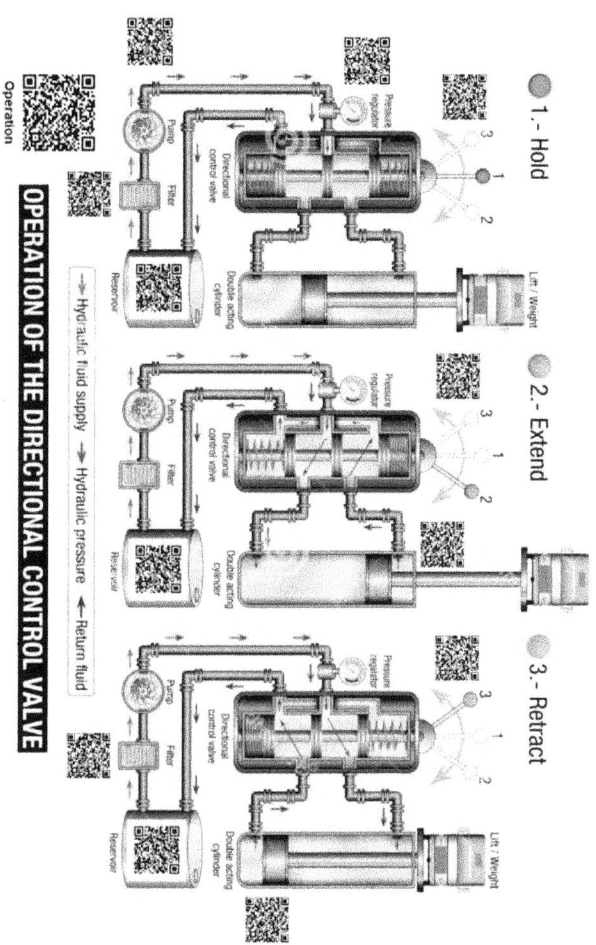
1.- Hold
2.- Extend
3.- Retract
Pressure regulator
Directional control valve
Pump
Filter
Reservoir
Double acting cylinder
Lift / Weight
Hydraulic fluid supply
Hydraulic pressure
Return fluid
OPERATION OF THE DIRECTIONAL CONTROL VALVE
Operation

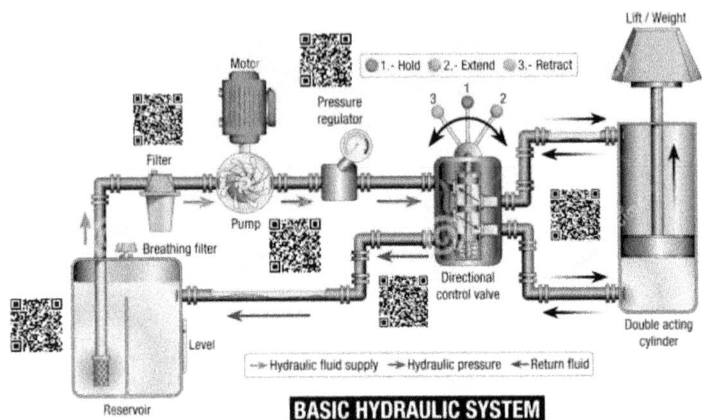

Direct Pressure Relief Valves

- The pressure relief valve provides protection against overload experienced by the actuators in a hydraulic system. One important function is to limit the force or torque produced by the hydraulic cylinders or motors.

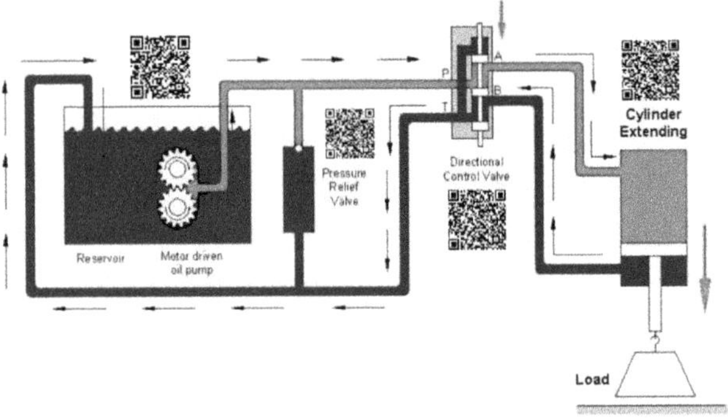

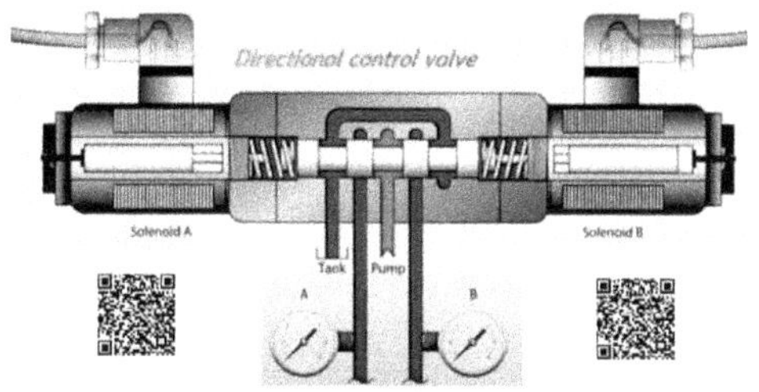

Double Acting, Single ended Cylinder

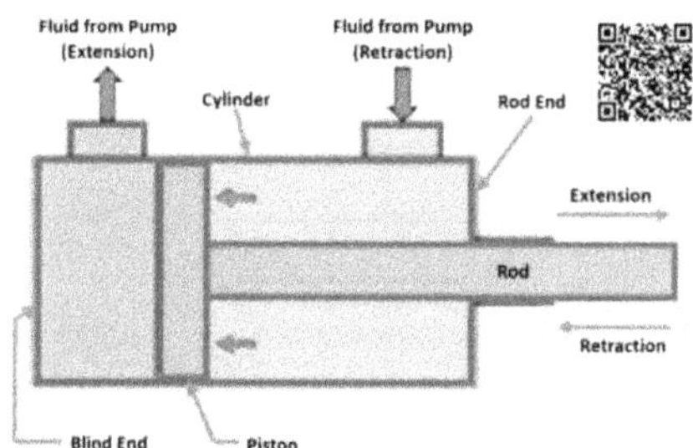

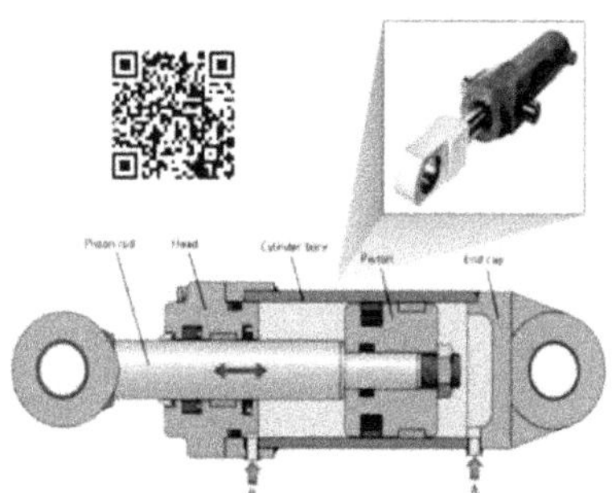

Hydraulic Cylinder

FLOW CONTROL VALVES

- A flow control valve can regulate the flow or pressure of the fluid.
- The fluid flow is controlled by varying area of the valve opening through which fluid passes.

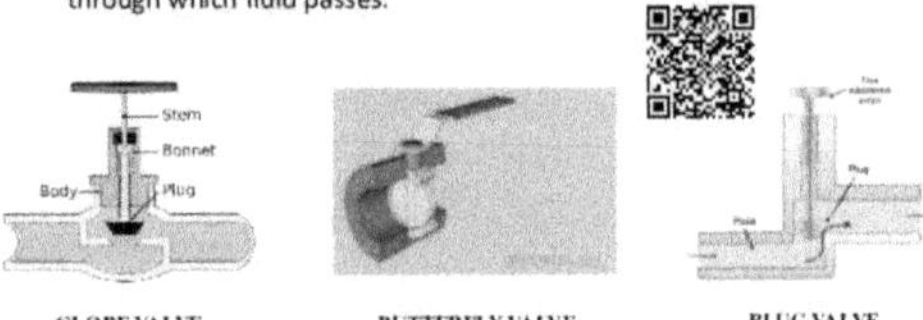

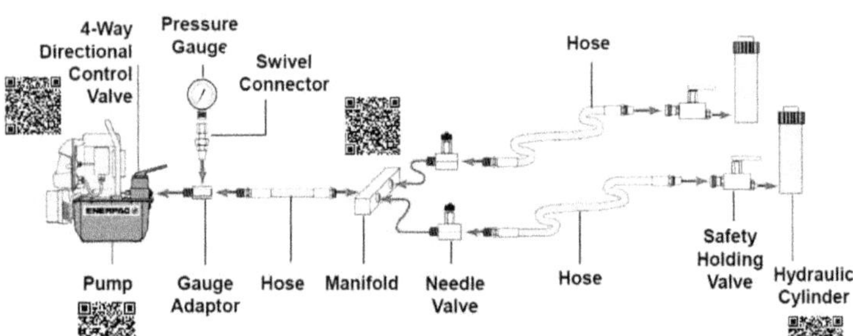

Hydraulic Multipoint System

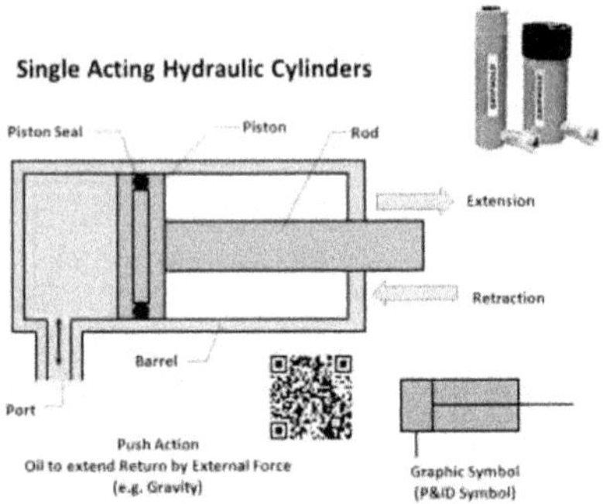

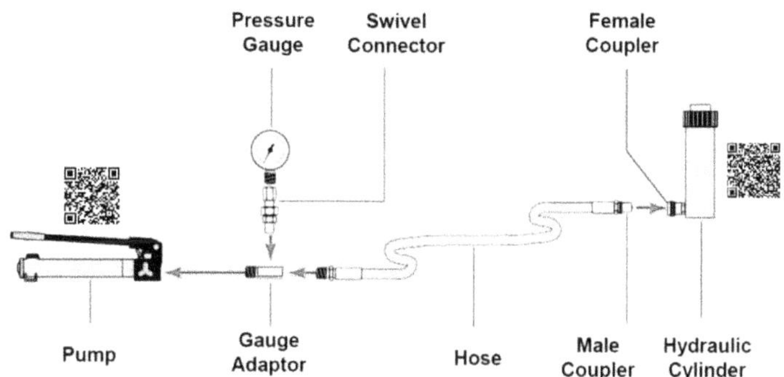

Hydraulic Single Point System

Types of Hydraulic Valves

- **Directional Control Valve:**
  Control the direction of flow of the hydraulic fluid to different lines in the circuit
- **Flow Control Valves:**
  Control the amount of fluid flow in the circuit
- **Pressure Control Valves:**
  Control the pressure in different segments in the circuit

Hydraulic Valves - Parts and Components

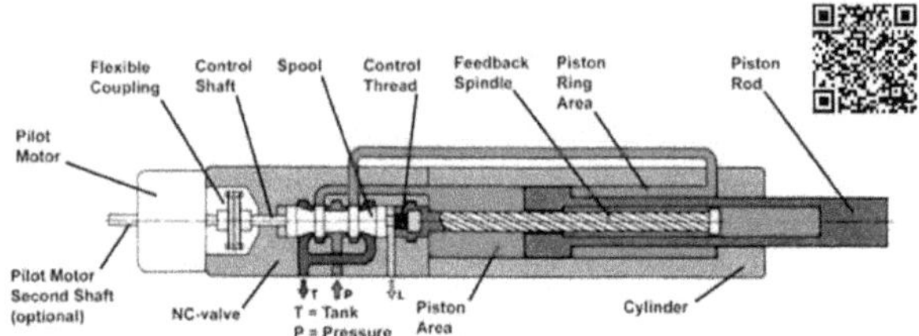

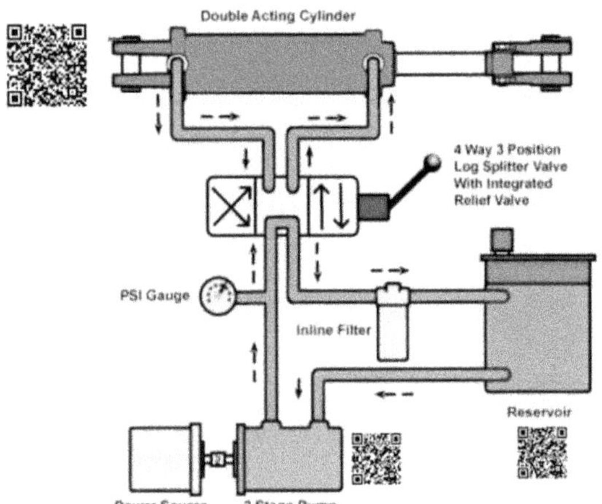

Hydraulic Double Acting Cylinder

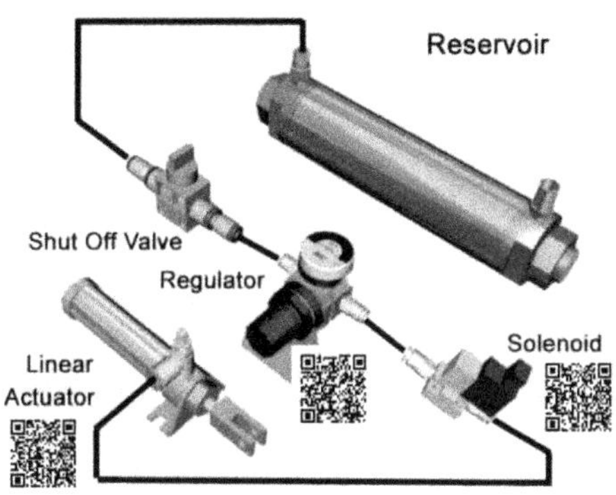

Pneumatic System

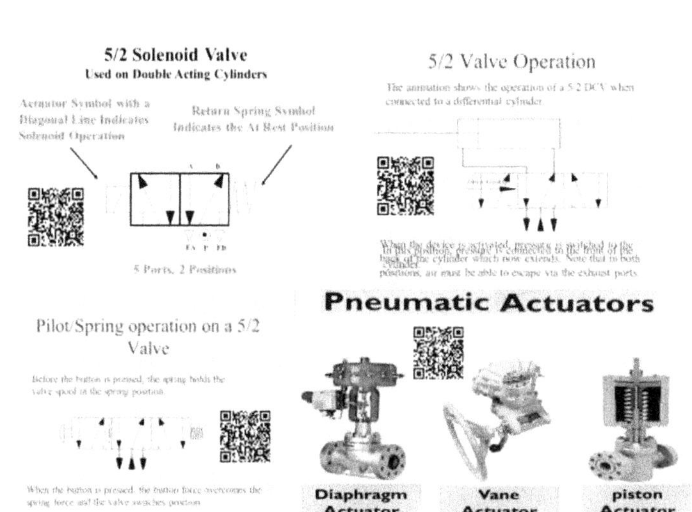

Pneumatic Control Valve **Pneumatic Control Valve Mechanisem**

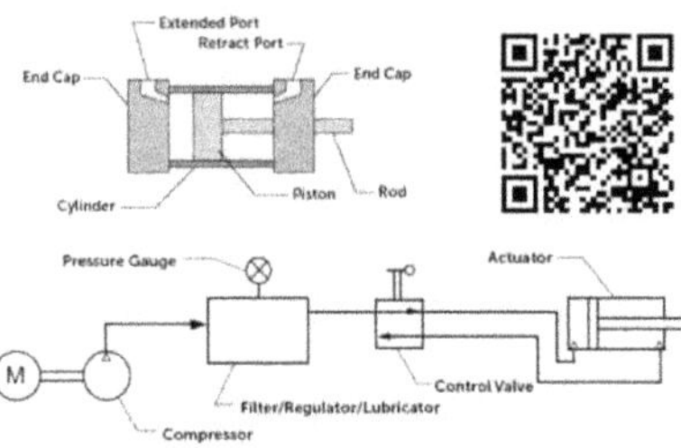

Pneumatic Cylinder System

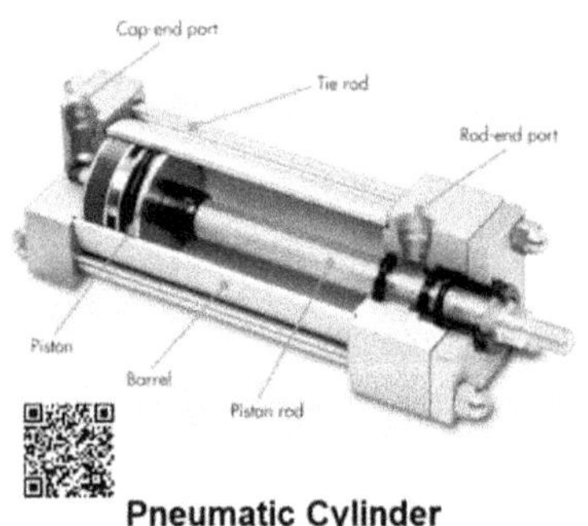

Pneumatic Cylinder

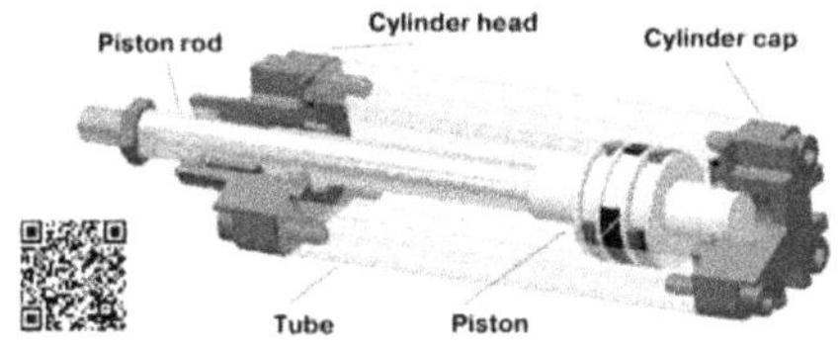
Pneumatic Cylinder
Piston rod
Cylinder head
Cylinder cap
Tube
Piston

2-way, 2-position, normally closed direct-acting solenoid valve, spring return

4-way (5-port), 2-position, piloted solenoid valve, spring return
A B
R P S

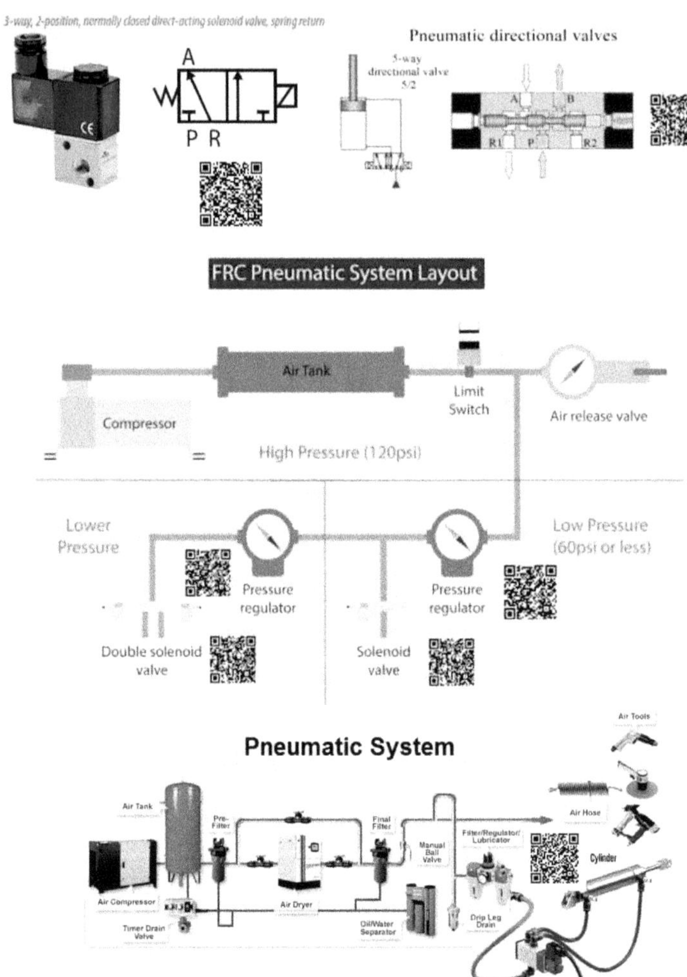
3-way, 2-position, normally closed direct-acting solenoid valve, spring return
A
P R
Pneumatic directional valves
5-way
directional valve
5/2
A
B
R1
P
R2
FRC Pneumatic System Layout
Air Tank
Compressor
Limit
Switch
Air release valve
High Pressure (120psi)
Lower
Pressure
Pressure
regulator
Pressure
regulator
Low Pressure
(60psi or less)
Double solenoid
valve
Solenoid
valve
Pneumatic System
Air Tools
Air Tank
Pre-
Filter
Final
Filter
Manual
Ball
Valve
Filter/Regulator/
Lubricator
Air Hose
Cylinder
Air Compressor
Air Dryer
Timer Drain
Valve
Oil/Water
Separator
Drip Leg
Drain
Valve

CHAPTER FIVE

Aeronautical Engineering MCQ

Safety Precaution in Aeronautical Engineering

01] In case of bleeding, take treatment Of

A] spray cold water

B] Bandage immediately -----]

C] Enquire about the accident thought treatment

D] cold 3" and rest

02] in case of an accident, the victim should im

A] Asked to take rest

C] Attended immediately

D] leave him

03] First aid is given to an injured or ill person primarily....

A] Save life

B] Prevent further deterioration of the muff's

C] Give best possible comfort

D] All of these

04] Colour code for Bins for waste paper segregation is -----

A] blue Colour

B] Yellow Colour

C] Red Colour

D] Green Colour

05] In Japanese Seiko stands for --------------

A] Shine

B] Sort

C] Standardize

D] Sustain

06] Benefit of SS system is ------

A] Increase in productivity
B] Increase in quality
C] Reduction in wastage of time
D] All of these

07] Safety is -----------
A] nobody's business
B] every bodise business
C] Some bodies business
D] The organization business

08] For basic categories of safety signs are available The meaning of"prohibition" sign ----
A] shows it must not be done
B] Shows what must be done
C] Warns the hazard or danger
D] Gives information of safety provision

09] Which one is a workshop safety?
A] Keep shop floor clean and free from grease, oil or other slippery materials
B] Stop the machine before changing the speed
C] Don't use cracked or chipped tools
D] Don't try to stop a running machine with hand

10] In Personal Protect Equipment (PPE] HELMET is used to
A] protect head
B] Protect eyes
C] Protect hands
D] Protect ears

11] Which of the following belongs to general safety?
A Have a worker in good attitude
B] The work clean and clear
C] Concentrate on your work
D] Keep the floor and gangways clean and clear

12] While grinding, which is used to protect the eyes?
A] Dark green glass
B] Mask
C] Sun glasses
D] Safety goggles

13] Which of the following is done for machine safety?
A] Check the oil level before starting the machine

B] Do things in a methodical way

C] Keep the floor and gangways clean and clear

D] Don't use dies and scarves

14] In Personal Protect Equipment (PPE], 'sleeves' is used to protect ----------

A] Face

B] Eyes

C] Ears

D] Hands

15] ABC stands for --------------

A] Automatic Breathing Control

B] Automatic Blood Control

C] Airway Breathing Circulation

D] Automatic Blood Circulation

16] To put off"Class B" fire, the types of fire extinguisher used is ....]

A] dry power

B] Carbon dioxide

C] Jet of water

D] Foam type

17] Which type of fire extinguisher is used to put off general fire?

A] Water type Extinguisher

B] Foam type Extinguisher

C] Dry chemical powder Extinguisher

D] Carbon dioxide (C02] Extinguisher

Hand Tools in Aeronautical Engineering

18] One micrometer (U] is equal to...

A] 0.1mm

B] 0.01mm

C] 0.001mm

D] 0.0001mm

19] Name the tool used to make and finish the leak proof joints of a pipe T joint

A] groover

B] setting hammer

C] creasing hammer

D] round bottom stake

20] Portion of the hammer used for fixing the handle is...

A] Face

B] Peen

C] Cheek

D] Eye hole

21] Weight of the hammer for the marking purpose is...

A] 250g

B] 500g

C] 1 kg

D] 2 kgs

22] To cut out small apertures which punch and die type of machine is used?

A] shear type nibbler

B] punch type nibbler

C] circular cutting machine

D] guillotine shearing machine

23] Scribers are made of...

A] Mild steel

B] High carbon steel

C] Brass

D] Cast iron

24] The size of an engineer's vice is specified by the...

A] Length of the movable jaw

B] Width of the jaws

C] Height of the vice

D] Maximum opening of the jaws

Bench Vice

25] The form of thread used in carpenters vice is...

A] Square

B] Acme thread

C] Sawtooth Thread

D] Knuckle thread

26] The convexity of files helps...

A] To file concave surfaces

B] To file convex surfaces

C] To prevent rounding of edges of work

D] The file to become straight when pressure is applied

27]] Name the instrument used to check the perpendicularity of the branch pipe with the main pipe of a pipe T joint

A] protractor

B] try square

C] spirit level

D] straight edge

28] The caliper meant for measuring the width of a slot is...

A] Odd leg caliper

B] Outside caliper

C] Jenny caliper

D] Inside calliper

29] The included angle of the groove of 'V' block is always....

A] 45◦

B] 60◦

C] 90◦

D] 120◦

'V' blocks

30] 'V' blocks are available in grades of...

A] A & B

B] A,B & C

C] 1,2 & 3

D] 1 & 2

31] 'V' blocks of grade 'B' are made of

A] Cast iron

B] Mild steel

C] Steel

D] Cast steel

32] 'V' block 50/5-40 A is used for holding jobs of diameter

A] Ø 50 mm

B] Ø 5 to Ø 50 mm

C] Ø 5 to Ø 40 mm

D] Ø 40 mm

33] The reason for using cast iron in making 'V' blocks

A] to increase the weight of the block

B] to reduce the cost

C] to reduce the friction

D] to get a good appearance

34] For cutting thin tubing, the most suitable pitch of the hacksaw blade is...

A] 1.8mm

B] 1.4mm

C] 1mm

D] 0.8mm

35] For cutting solid brass, the most suitable pitch of the hacksaw blade is...

A] 1.8mm

B] 1.4mm

C] 1mm

D] 0.8mm

36] A new hacksaw blade after a few strokes becomes loose because of the...

A] Stretching of the blade

B] Wing-nut threads being worn out

C] Wrong pitch of the blade

D] Improper selection of the set of saws.

37] While cutting small diameter pipes, it is advisable to watch regularly and ensure that...

A] The cut is along the curved line

B] More saw teeth are in contract

C] The work is not overheated

D] Proper balancing of hacksaw is maintained

Drilling in Aeronautical Engineering

38] If the drill runs untrue, it will

A] get too hot

B] cut undersize

C] distort the spindle

D] cut an oversized hole

39] Running the drill too fast many result in

A] spoiling the cutting edge

B] poor surface finish

C] twisting the tang

D] drilling an oval hole

40] A drill with worn land will
A] drill hole oversize
B] drill hole undersize
C] run out of centre
D] drill an accurate hole
41] The morse taper provided on drills used on lathe ranges between
A] MT1 to MT5
B] MT1 to MT4
C] MT0 to MT5
D] MT0 to MT4
42] Feeding the small drill too fast into the work may result in
A] breaking the drill
B] bending the drill
C] cutting an oval shape hole
D] increased production
43] The drill size for a M 20 tap is
A] 17.5 mm
B] 18 mm
C] 18.5 mm
D] 19 mm
44] The taper shank drills are held on the machine by means of...
A] Chucks
B] Sleeves
C] Drift
D] Vice
45] Drill chucks are fitted on the drilling machine spindle by means of a...
A] Knurled ring
B] Arbor
C] Drift
D] Pinion and key

Drill Chuck

46] The Morse taper provided on drills ranges between...

A] MT 1 to MT 5

B] MT 1 to MT 4

C] MT 0 to MT 5

D] MT 0 to MT 4

47] A drift is used for...

A] Drawing a drill location

B] Fixing chuck on the machine spindle

C] Removing a broken drill from the work

D] Removing the drill from the machine spindle

48] When the taper shank of the drill is larger than the machine spindle, the device to hold the drill is a...

A] Drill sleeve

B] Taper socket

C] Drill drift

D] Chuck and key

49] A special feature of the radial drilling machine is...

A] It can be used for drilling with a H.S.S] drill
B] Table can be moved and set at any position
C] A variety of speeds is available
D] The spindle can be brought to any position
50] The point angle of drills depends on...
A] The size of the drill
B] The type of machine
C] The material of the work
D] The RPM of the drill
51] The point angle for a standard drill is...
A] 60°
B] 108°
C] 118°
D] 135°
52] The helical angle determines the...
A] Cutting angle
B] Chew angle
C] Rake angle
D] Lip angle
53] The clearance angle of the drill is between...
A] 3° to 5°
B] 8° to 12°
C] 12° to 20°
D] 15° to 20°
54] The relief angle provided behind the cutting edge is called the..
A] Point angle
B] Chisel edge angle
C] Helix angle
D] Clearance angle
55] A set of number drill series consists of drills in the following ranges] Indicate the correct range
A] 1 to 40
B] 1 to 50
C] 1 to 80
D] 1 to 100
56] In the number drill series, the smallest drill size is...
A] 0.1 mm

B] 0.35 mm
C] 0.5 mm
D] 0.52 mm
57] In the number drill series, the largest drill size is...
A] 102 mm
B] 5.791 mm
C] 5.613 mm
D] 5.410 mm
58] In the letter drill series, the size of the drill 'A' is equal to ...
A] 13 mm
B] 6.08 mm
C] 6.045 mm
D] 5.944 mm
59] In the letter drill series, the largest drill size is equal to...
A] 10.33 mm
B] 10.490 mm
C] 12.01 mm
D] 15.00 mm
60] In a remote place (no electricity available] a rail track is to be drilled] Choose the right drilling machine
A] Radial drilling machine
B] Pillar drilling machine
C] Ratchet drilling machine
D] Sensitive drilling Machine
61] A drilling machine used by a carpenter for cabinet making is a...
A] Ratchet drilling machine
B] Radial drilling machine
C] Breast drilling machine
D] Sensitive drilling machine
62] Surface plates are made of...
A] High grade cast steel
B] Fine-grained cast iron
C] Alloy steels
D] Wrought iron
63] The drill size for a M 20 tap is
A] 17.5 mm
B] 18 mm
C] 18.5 mm

D] 19 mm

64] Tapping is mostly done to produce

A] external 'V' thread

B] <u>internal 'V' thread</u>

C] external square thread

D] internal square thread

65] The drill size for tapping is

A] more than the tap size

B] <u>less than the tap size</u>

C] equal to the tap size

D] either more or less than the tap size

66] which one of the following is the most suitable tap for lathe work?

A] spiral tap

B] <u>machine tap</u>

C] hand tap

D] left hand tap

67] A die is turned with a

A] die wrench

B] <u>diestock</u>

C] die plate

D] die handle

68] A tumbler gear unit has

A] a single gear

B] two gears

C] <u>three gears</u>

D] four gears

69] The cutting edge of a solid tool is made of

A] <u>carbon steel</u>

B] mild steel

C] super high speed steel

D] stelite

70] The tip of a cemented carbide threading tool is

A] <u>brazed</u>

B] welded

C] soldered

D] clamped to the shank

71] Tool will rub against the work surfaces and the cutting force increases when..

A] The clearance angle is more
B] The clearance angel is less
C] The rake angle is more
D] The rake angle is less
72] Formation of a chip while cutting is based on the...
A] Rake angle of the tool
B] Clearance angle of the tool
C] Wedge angle of the tool
D] Clearance and wedge angle of the tool
73] The suitable cutting fluid for drilling mild steel in a drilling machine is...
A] Synthetic soluble oil
B] Neat oil
C] Distilled water
D] Soluble oil
74] Centre drilling is an operation of...
A] Drilling and countersinking
B] Drilling and counter boring
C] Marking the centre location before drilling
D] Enlarging the diameter of a hole
75] Shaft ends are centre drilled for...
A] Supporting jobs between centres
B] Lubricating the dead centre
C] Reducing the weight
D] Assisting counter boring
76] The Centre drill size is selected on the basis of the
A] length of the job
B] material of the job
C] diameter of the job
D] type of operation
77] Centre drilling is done at a
A] high spindle speed with a high feed
B] low spindle speed with a high feed
C] high spindle speed with a low feed
D] low spindle speed with a low feed

Measuring Instruments in Aeronautical Engineering

78] The least count of vernier caliper is
A] 0.01 mm

B] 0.02mm

C] 0.001 mm

D] 0.2 mm

Vernier Caliper

79] The graduations of a depth micrometer are...

A] Similar to an outside micrometer

B] In the reverse direction to that of the outside micrometer, both Thimble and sleeve

C] In the reverse direction only on the sleeve

D] In the direction only on the thimble

Depth Micrometer

80] The process of enlarging the end of a hole for accommodating the socket screw head is...

A] Reaming

B] Spot facing

C] Counter boring

D] Counter sinking

Boring Operation

81]While choosing a boring tool for boring a given diameter, select

A] a long tool

B] a short tool

C] a long and stout tool

D] a short and stout tool

82] The cutting edge of the boring tool should be set for a small hole so that it is

A] 0.5 mm above the center

B] 0.5 mm below the center

C] 1 mm above the center

D] in the exact center

83] Bored holes are to be chamfered by using

A] a drill

B] triangular scraper

C] a cranked boring tool

D] a flat file

84] The tool used for boring deep holes is a

A] lathe mandrel

B] sleeve

C] drill

D] boring bar

E] auger bit

85] The cutting speed for rough boring is the

A] same as rough turning

B] same as drilling

C] same as knurling

D] same as thread cutting

86] The reamer is used for...

A] Drilling holes in thin sheets

B] Drilling deep holes

C] Removing burrs

D] Enlarging and finishing holes

Reamer

87] The reamer teeth are unevenly spaced because...

A] They are easy to manufacture

B] They can reduce chattering

C] They help to cut metal gradually

D] They help to remove the reamer easily

88] Which among the following is not a capability of reamers?

A] Finishing small holes

B] Finishing any machined profiles

C] Accuracy to closer limits

D] Producing high quality surface finish

89] The most important quality of any cutting fluid is

A] emulsification

B] specific heat

C] specific gravity

D] viscosity

Cutting Fluid

90] By using coolants on workpieces we can choose

A] higher cutting speeds

B] lower cutting feeds

C] lower cutting speeds

D] heavy depth of cuts

91] The cutting speed for aluminium with H.S.S] tools is

A] 30 m/min

B] 50 m/min

C] 70 m/min

D] 130 m/min

92] The cutting speed for brass with a H.S.S] tool is

A] 10 m/min

B] 25 m/min

C] 70 m/min

D] 140 m/min

93] The distance, which the cutting edge of a tool passes over the material in a minute while machining is Know as...

A] RPM

B] Feed

C] Machine speed

D] Cutting speed

94] The cutting angle for chipping cast iron is...

A] 37.5°

B] 55°

C] 60°

D] 90°

95] The depth of cut is given by

A] the top slide
B] <u>the cross-slide</u>
C] the compound slide
D] adjusting the tool
96] For mounting a lathe chuck
A] start it by hand and then turn the power on
B] mount it on by power
C] <u>mount it by hand</u>
D] mount it with the help of a hammer

Lathe Four Jaw Chuck

97] The morse taper provided on drills used on lathe ranges between
A] <u>MT1 to MT5</u>
B] MT1 to MT4
C] MT0 to MT5
D] MT0 to MT4
98] Feeding the small drill too fast into the work may result in
A] <u>breaking the drill</u>
B] bending the drill

C] cutting an oval shape hole

D] increased production

99] Number of flutes in a twist drills are --------

A] 1

B] 2

C] 3

D] 4

100] Which one of the following drilling machines is used for drilling holes where electricity is not available?

A] Bench drilling machine

B] Pillar drilling machine

C] Redial drilling machine

D] Ratchet drilling machine

101] Which one of the following drilling machine is used for heavy duty work?

A] Bench drilling machine

B] Pillar drilling machine

C] Radial drilling machine

D] Electric hand drilling machine

102] The suitable cutting fluid for drilling mild steel in a lathe is

A] synthetic soluble oil

B] neat cutting oil

C] distilled water

D] soluble oil+water

103] The suitable cutting fluid for precision grinding is

A] Soluble oil

B] Synthetic soluble oil

C] Neat oil

D] Servo Cut's'

Grinding Wheel

104] Advantage of using cutting fluid during grinding operation is ------

A] 5000 surface finish

B] Reduction in cutting forces

C] Reduction in hardening of the work piece

D] All of these]

105] Lubricant is necessary to ....]

A] run the machine smoothly taking least load

B] Run the machine quickly

C] Stop the machine immediately

D] Produce work piece of greater accuracy

106] The main purpose for using a lubricant in machine tools is to ------

A] Cool down the making parts

B] Prevent machine tool from heating

C] Wet the making parts for close contact

D] Minimize the friction between the making parts

107] Driving plates are used for

A] mounting fixtures and workpieces

B] driving shafts between Centre's with a lathe dog

C] facing operations only

D] internal operations only

108] Balancing is done in the face plate work

A] to increase the speed

B] to reduce the pressure on the tool

C] for uniform rotation of work

D] to get a good finish

109] A face plate is used to hold

A] a round job

B] a finished job

C] an irregular Job

D] a hollow job

110] Which is correct angle plate used with face plate

(A] Solid Type

(B] Box Type

(C] Adjustable Type

(D] None of them

Angle Plate

111] Face plate is made from.....]

(A] Mild Steel

(B] Cast Iron

(C] Brass

(D] Aluminium

112] Which following accessories is use for odd an uneven job turning?

(A] Three Jaw Chuck

(B] Two Jaw Chuck

(C] Driving Plate

(D] Face Plate

113] An irregular shaped work piece is turned on a Lathe] Which one of the following work holding accessories is used?

A] Two Jaw chuck

B] Three Jaw chuck

C] Driving plate

D] Face plate

114]The pads of a steady rest are made of

A] carbon steel

B] lead

C] mild steel

D] brass

Steady Rest

115] A steady rest is used

A] to hold jobs

B] for face plate work

C] to drive the job

D] to support the job

116] A follower steady is held on the

A] lathe bed

B] lathe carriage

C] lathe spindle

D] tailstock

117] When turning long work pieces, the following is used

A sleeve

B change gear

C steady rest

D bracket]

118] Knurling operation is done at the

A] turning spindle speed

B] high spindle speed

C] 1/3 of the turning spindle speed

D] 1⁄2 of the turning spindle speed

Knurling Tool

119] Knurling is the operation of

A] shearing

B] forming

C] turning

D] pressing

120] Mandrels are generally used when machining with

A] heavy cuts

B] short facing cuts

C] light cuts

D] boring tools

Limit Fit & Tolerances in Aeronautical Engineering

121] In the B.I.S system 25 hole deviations are specified by

A] small letters

B] small letters with numbers

C] small letters with tolerance

D] capital letters

122] The standard range of sizes covered in the B.I.S] system of limits and fits are

A] 0 to 10 mm

B] 0 to 100 mm

C] 25 to 400 mm

D] 0 to 500 mm

123] The basic size is the size

A] mentioned in the drawing

B] machined by the operator

C] based on which deviations are given

D] given by the instructor

124] Limits of size are

A] 2

B] 3

C] 4

D] 5

125] The number of fundamental deviations in the B.I.S] system are

A] 20

B] 22

C] 25

D] 28

126] The number of grade of tolerances in the B.I.S] system are

A] 12

B] 16

C] 18

D] 20

127] The size based on which the dimensional deviations are given is called...

A] Actual size

B] Basic size

C] Minimum limit of size

D] Maximum limit of Size

128] The size of parts made by .....] for provide interchange ability properties] (A] Measurement System

(B] Trial and Error System

(C] Limit and Tolerance System

(D] None of Them

129] Your job taper is correct if it is measured

A above the higher limit

B in between higher and lower limit

C below the lower limit]

130] When tolerance given in one side of the basic dimension, it is called --------

A].Tolerance system

B] Unilateral tolerance

C] Bilateral tolerance

D] Allowance System

131] A dimension is stated as (025 H7 in a drawing] The lower limit is -----------

A] 24.75 mm

B] 24.85 mm

C] 25.00 mm

D] 25-021 mm

132] The measured Size Of the dimensions of a component as called---------

A] Basic size

B] Nominal Size

C] Allowed size

D] Actual size

133] In the drawing the dimensions of a shaft is shown 40i 0068/0042, which is the size of Shaft within the tolerance?

A] 4.0.64 mm

B] 40.042 mm

C] 40.000 mm

D] 39.998 mm

134] In Hole basic system ----------

A] The size of the shaft is made constant

B] The Size of the hole is made constant

C] Only 'allowance is given on the hole

D] The permissible tolerance are given on the hole and the Shaft

135] The Size of a component is given as 24 -0.1] What does -O.1 indicates? _

A] Upper deviation is + 0.1 mm]

B] Lower deviation is 0.0 mm

C] Fundamental deviation is 0.0 mm

D] Lower deviation is _0.1 mm

136] The tolerance of a hole iS the difference between the -------

A] Maximum hole Size and maximum Shaft size

B] Maximum hole size and maximum hole Size

C] Minimum'hole size and maximum Shaft Size

D] Minimum hole Size and minimum shaft Size

137] A hole whose lower deviation is zero is called basic hole] Which one of the following letter indicates basic hole?]

A] E

B] F

C] G '

D] H

138] Which one having upper deviation zero?

A] Bassc Shaft

B] Basic hole

C] Tolerance

D] Clearance

139] A ball bearing on a shaft is type of fit? ,

A] Clearance fit

B] Driving fit

C] Shrinkage fit

D] None of the above

140] Which one of the following is important factor required to achieve the interchange ability in mass production?]

A] Geometrical accuracy]

B] Standardization

C] Dimensional accuracy

D] Surface finish

141] In the BIS system of limits and fits, the grade of tolerance are represented by number Symbols and there are ---------i

A] 14 grades of tolerance

B] 16 grades of tolerance

C] 18 grades of tolerance ‘

D] 20 grades of tolerance

142] A Product is said to have the quality when ....]

A] Its shape and dimensions are within the limit

B] It is fit for use

C] It appears to be very good

D] The choice of material is right

143] The maximum clearance required between hole’30 +0.021, 0.000 and shaft 30 -0.110, 0.143 is.

A] 0.110 mm ‘

B]0.131 mm

C] 0.164 mm

D] 0.143 mm

144] A dimension is stated as 25 .1002 mm in a drawing] What is the tolerance?

A] +0.02 mm’

B] +0.04 mm

C] -0.02 mm

D] 25.00 mm

145] A pin is fitted in a hole] The tolerance zone of the pin is entirely above that of hole] The fit obtained will be?

A] Clearance fit

B] Transition fit

C] Interference fit

D] Running fit

146] Interchange ability is normally applied for? _

A] Repairing of parts

B] Mass production

C] Single piece production

D] All of these

147] Tolerance is given to the part size to...........]

A] Production the part within the required permissible size error

B] Increase the production

C] Decrease the Production

D] Finish the components approximately

148] Which one of the following is the clearance fit under the whole basic system?

A] 20 H7/p6'

B] 2067/211

C] ZOG/gll]

D] 20H/g11]

149] The three classes of fits as per BIS system aré ....] ~]

A] Clearance fit, interference fit and transition fit

B] Medium fit, push fit and tight fit

C] Flat fit, round fit and square fit

D] 'Sliding fit ', loose fit and shrinkage fit

150] Which one of the following tolerance specifications has a maximum dimensionless than 20 mm?

A] 20 +0.2,-0.3

B] 20 320.2

C] 20 -0.2, 0.3 e

D]m 20 +500, ~03

151] Difference between the maximum and minimum limit is -~-~~~~-~~~~~ '

A] Single informant

B] Basic shaft

C] Clearance

D] Tolerance

152] A shaft 55 running freely in bush bearing the type of fit is ---------

A] Clearance fit

B] Driving plate

C] shrinkage fit

D] None of the above

153] The taper ratio of the morse taper is

A] 1 in 10

B] 1 in 15

C] 1 in 20

D] 1 in 25

154] The morse standard taper is available in

A] 16 Nos

B] 12 Nos

C] 10 Nos

D] 8 Nos

155] Taper turning by offsetting the tailstock method can produce

A] an internal taper

B] an internal taper thread

C] an external taper

D] both external and internal tapers

Taper by Tailstock Offset

156] By using the taper turning attachment, tapers can be turned with a setting angle up to

A] 10°

B] 15°

C] 20°

D] 30◦

157] The accuracy of a taper is generally checked by means of......

A] taper gauges

B] gauge blocks

C] indicator and height gauge

D] 'V' blocks

158] Turning tapers by the compound rest method involves working solely with

Decimal measurements

B fractional measurements

C metric measurements

D angular measurements]

159] Long tapers are produced

A with the taper turning attachment

B with the compound slide

C by setting over the tail stock

D by adjusting the cross slide]

160] The length of turned tapers are checked with

A vernier calliper

B micrometer

C inside callper

D dial test indicator]

161] The disadvantages of taper turning using the com] pound slide are

A] only long tapers can be turned

B] only very large tapers can be turned

C] only manual in feed is possible

D] only short tapers can be turned due to the restrictions of the compound slide]

162] External tapers are checked with

A] limit plug gauge

B] taper ring gauge

C]taper plug gauge

D] thread plug gauge]

163] The use of a taper turned on lathe is ----

A] Assist to transmit drive in the assembled parts

B] Used for Assembly and disassembly of parts

C] Give self alignment in the assembled parts

164] Which type of method is used in mass production of production of producing small length of taper?

A] Form tool

B] Compound slide

C] Tailstock offset.

D] Taper turning attachment

165] Morse standard taper is one of the internationally accepted standards taper, which is available in numbers from--------

A]1to7

B]1 to 8

C] O to 7

D] 0 to 8

166] Which taper turning method is used for cutting steep taper?

A] Set over method

B] Taper turning attachment

C] Form tool

D] Swivelling the compound rest

167] Morse taper is used in which of the following machine components -...

A] Spindles of lathe

B] Spindles of drill machine

C] Shanks of reamers

D] All of these

168] For mass production of the taper which one of the following method is used.......]

A] Tailstock offset method

B] Taper turning attachment method

C] Form too method

D] Compound slide method

169] The major diameter of the taper is 40 mm, minor diameter is 30 mm] The total length of the job is 100 mm is tapered then offset is given by -

A] 5 mm

B] 7.5 mm

C] 12 mm

D] 9 mm

170] The accuracy of an ordinary bevel protractor is --' ------------degree]

A] One

B] Three

C] Two

D] Four

171] The least count of a vernier bevel protractor is...

A] 1”

B] 5’

C] 1◦

D] 5 ◦

172] The part of a vernier bevel protractor which is normally used as a reference base for measuring angles is the...

A] Blade

B] Stock

C] Disc

C] Main scale

173] The part of a vernier bevel protector on which main scale divisions are marked is the...

A] Stock

B] Dial

C] Disc

D] Adjustable blade

174] The part of a bevel protractor, which comes in contact with the inclined surface while measuring is the...

A] Blade

B] Stock

C] Disc

D] Dial

175] The value of each division of the main scale of a vernier bevel protractor is...

A] 5’

B] 1◦

C] 5◦

D.10◦

176] The value of each division of the vernier scale of a bevel protractor is...

A] 1◦

B] 1◦5’

C] 1◦55’

D.5'

177] The part of the vernier bevel protractor on which main scale divisions are marked

A stock

B dial

C disc

D adjustable blade

178] In Vernier bevel protractor is designed to measure?

A] Acute angles

B] Obtuse angles

C] Acute and Obtuse angle

D] Liner dimensions

179] To get least count of 5 in a vernier bevel protractor the 23° main scale are divided into -..

A] 12 equal parts on vernier scale

B] 22 equal parts on vernier scale

C] 24 equal parts on vernier scale

D] 25 equal parts on vernier scale

180] Which of the following is not the part of a combination set?

A] Stock

B] Square head

C] Protractor head

D] Centre head

181] The datum, form which the measurements of the vernier height gauge are taken, is...

A] The beam

B] The vernier slide

C] The base

D] Above the scriber poing

Vernier Height Gauge

182]The part of a vernier height gauge on which the main scale divisions are graduated is the...

A] Base

B] Beam

C] Fine setting device

D] The vernier plate

183] On which part of the vernier height gauge are the main scale division graduated?]

A] Base

B] Vernier plate

C] Beam

D] Fine adjusting unit

184] For marking purpose a Vernier height gauge must be on the --------

A] Bed of a machine tool

B] Surface plate

C] Square block

D] Any flat surface

185] Before using Vernier height gauge make sure that the --------

A] Locking screw is in a locked position

B] Scriber is Locked

C] Zero of the vernier coincides with zero of the main scale

D] Gib is Provided

186] The least count Of a vernier height gauge is...........]

A] 0.05 mm

B] 0.1 mm

C] 0.02 mm

D] 0001 mm

187] Which laying out the vernier height gauge must be used on the ----------

A] V block

B] Machine bed

C] Surface plate

D] Any flat surface

188] The part which is slides on the beam of a vernier height gauge is known as a ------

A] Base

B] Beam scale

C] Scriber

D] Vernier slide

189] The base of the vernier height gauge is generally made out of ---------

A] Cast iron]

B] Steel

C] Aluminium alloy

D] Tungsten carbide

190] Which instrument iis used for marking layout?

A] Micrometer

B] Vernier

C] Depth gauge

D] Vernier height gauge

191] While marking with a Vernier height gauge, the work piece is generally ----------

A] Supported by an angle plate

B] Supported by another work piece

C] Held by one hand

D] Held without support

192] Which of the following is not the part of a combination set?

A] Stock

B] Square head

C] Protractor head

D] Centre head

Engineering Drawing in Aeronautical Engineering

18]The 'T' square is used for drawing lines ......

a] inclined

b] curved

c] vertical
d] horizontal
19] For drawing large size circle is drawn by.....
a] straight bar
b] lengthening bar
c] big bar
d] small bar
20] To draw or measure angle is used by.....
a]set square
b] protractor
c] 'T' square
d] none of these
21] The grade of pencil is used to sketching lettering ....
a] conical point
b] chisel point
c] soft
d] low
22] For drawing thin lines of uniform thickness the pencil should be sharpened in the form of ....
a] chisel edge
b]conical
c] pointed
d] none of these
23] What is used for drawing curves which can not drawn by compass
a] small compass
b] French curve
c] protractor
d] none of these
24]Unnecessary lines is removed by .....
a] Duster
b] sand paper block
c] eraser
d] none of these
25] Circle and arcs are drawn by means of .....l.
a] compass
b] divider
c] lengthening bar
d]none of these

26] Inking pen is used in drawing ......
a] horizontal line
b] non circular arcs
c] vertical lines
d] all of these
27] The card board scale are available in set of .....
a] 7
b] 8
c] 6
d] 9
28] The convenient length size of 30 -60°-90° set square for used in school and colleges are......
a] 250
b] 200
c] 300
d] none of these
29] Drawing board is shape of ....
a] square
b] rectangular
c] triangular
d] none of these
30] The 'T' square , set square ,scale protractor are complain use in.......
a] protractor
b] mini drafter
c] set square
d] none of these
31]Set square , T square edges are bevelled for the purpose of....
a] curve line
b] inking lines
b] taking measurements
d] none of these
32]Geometrical construction which are mostly based on plane geometry and which are very.......
a] Accuracy
b] Quality
c] Essential
d] Superior quality
33] How much method of drawing the regular polygons.......

a] Inscribe circle method and arc method
b] General method for drawing any polygon
c] Alternative method
d] All of these

34] The line AB can be divided into .... equal parts.
a] 7
b] 10
c] 15
d] All of them

35] Which method of constructing triangl in circle......
a] Inscribing
b] Describing
c] Both a and b
d] None of these

36] When two sides of the hexagon are required to be horizontal the starting point for stepping equal division should be on an end of the.....
a] Horizontal diameter
b] Vertical diameter
c] Inclined diameter
d] None of these

37] If two sides of hexagon are required to be vertical the starting point should be on an end of the....
a] Inclined diameter
b] Horizontal diameter
c] Vertical diameter
d] None of these

38] The section obtained by the inter section of the right circular cone by a plane in different position relative to the axis of the cone are called.......
a] Conics
b] Circles
c] Triangles
d] Half circle

39] When the section plane is inclined to the axis and cuts all the generators on one side on a apex the section is in......
a] Conic section
b] Ellipse
c] Parabola
d] Hyperbola

40] When the section plane is inclined to the axis and is parallel to one of the generators the section is a ....

a] Ellipse

b] Parabola

c] Hyperbola

d] Cycloid

41] Use of elliptical curve is........

a] Arches

b] Dams and monuments

c] Manholes, gland & stuffing boxes

d] All of these

42] Use of parabolic curve is.........

a] Bridges & arches

b] Sound reflectors

c] Light reflectors

d] All of these

43] Use of hyperbolical curve is......

a] Cooling towers and water channel

b] Dames

c] Bridges

d] All of these

44] When the point is within the circle, the curve is called an.......

a] Superior trochoid

b] Interior trochoid

c] Trochoid

d] Isotrochoid

45] When the point outside the circle then the curve is called as......

a] Interior trochoid

b] Superior trochoid

c] Trochoid

d] Insuperior trochoid

46] The curve general by a point on a circumference of a circle, which rolls without slipping along another circle it is called.......

a] Epicycloids

b] Hypocycloid

c] Involute

d] None of these

47] When the circle rolls inside another circle the curve is called.......

a] Hypocycloid
b] Epicycloids
c] Trochoid
d] Hypotrochoid
48] The use of archemedian spiral curve is made in........
a] Teeth profiles of helical gears
b] Profiles of cams
c] Both a & b
d] None of these
49] The cams are widely used in........
a] Automates
b] Printing machines
c] C engines
d] All of these
50] Spring index =
a] Diameter of coil / diameter of a wire
b] Diameter of wire /diameter of coil
c] Mean diameter of wire / diameter of coil
d] Mean diameter of a coil / diameter of wire
51] Eccentricity =
a] Distance of a point from the focus / distance of the point from directrix
b] Distance of focus from point / distance of point from
c] Distance of point from focus / distance of directrix of point
d] Distance of point from directrix / distance of point from focus
52] Mathematically an ellipse can be described by equation.....
a] $a^2 / X^2 + y^2 / b^2 = 1$
b] $x^2 / a^2 + y^2 / b^2$
c] $x^2 / a^2 + y^2 / b^2 = 0$
d] $x^2 / a^2 + y^2 / b^2 = 1$
53] Mathematically a parabola can be described by an equation......
a] $y^2 = 4ax$
b] $x^2 = 2ay$
c] $x^2 = 4ay$
d] Both a & b
54] Mathematically hyperbola can be described by an equation.......
a] $x^2 /a^2 - y^2 /b^2 = 1$
b] $x^2 /y^2 - y^2 /x^2 = 0$

c] Both a & b

d] None of these

55] Cycloid can be described by an equation......

a] $y = a(1 - \cos Ø]$

b] $x = a(Ø - \sin Ø]$

c] <u>Both a & b</u>

d] None of these

56] The mathematically represented hypocycloid is.....

a] $Y = a \cos^3 Ø$, $X = a \sin^3 Ø$

b] $X = a \sin^3 Ø$, $Y = a \cos^3 Ø$

c] <u>$X = a \cos^3 Ø$, $Y = a \sin^3 Ø$</u>

d] None of these

57] Mathematically represented by involute is

a] $X = r \sin Ø - r Ø \cos Ø$, $Y = r \cos + r Ø \sin Ø$

b] $X = r \sin Ø + r \cos Ø$, $Y = r \cos Ø - r Ø \sin Ø$

c] $Y = r Ø \cos Ø - r \sin Ø$, $X = r \sin Ø - r Ø \cos Ø$

d] <u>$X = r \cos Ø + r Ø \sin Ø$, $Y = r \sin Ø - r Ø \cos Ø$</u>

58] The lines from the object to the plane are called.......

a] Projection

b] <u>Projector</u>

c] Reference plane

d] None of these

59] The orthographic projection an object is represented by View on the mutual perpendicular projection lines

a] <u>Two or three</u>

b] Three or two

c] Three or four

d] None of these

60] When the projectors are parallel to each other & also perpendicular to the plane, the projection is called......

a] Isometric projection

b] Oblique projection

c] <u>Orthographic projection</u>

d] Perspective projection

61] The two planes employed for the purpose of Orthographic projections are......

a] Auxillary plane

d] Horizontal plane

c] Reference plane

d] None of these

62] The line in which they intersect is termed the reference line & is denoted by the letters.......

a] AB

b] YZ

c] XY

d] None of these

63] The projection on the VP is called........

a] Side view

b] Front view

c] Top view

d] All of these

64] ....Method, when the views are drawn in their relative positions, the plane comes below the elevation. The view of the object as observed from the left-side the right of elevation.

a] Plane of projection

b] First angle projection

c] Third angle projection

d] None of these

65] Third angle projection method, the object is assumed to be situated in the........ quadrant.

a] First quadrant

b] Second quadrant

c] Third quadrant

d] Fourth quadrant

66] .... Method of projection is used in U.S.A & also in other countries.

a] plane of projection

b] Orthographic projection

c] First-angle projection

d] Third angle projection

67] When an object is situated on the ground, in first angle projection method, the bottom of its ..... will co-inside with XY

a] Top view

b] Front view

c] side view

d] All of these

68] The important element of this projection system

a] An object

b] Plane of projection

c] An observer

d] All of these

69] When line AB is parallel to HP hence ....

a] It' front view to AB

b] It''s side view equal to AB

c] It's top view equal to AB

d] None of these

70] When a line is parallel to a plane; it's projection on plane is equal to it's ;

a] True length

b] True shape

c] True size

d] None of these

71] The point is parallel in which the line or line produced meet the point is plane is called it's ....

a] Line

b] ratio

c] Trace

d] none of these

72] .... is the shortest distance between two points.

a] a line

b] a point

c] a straight line

d] none of these

73] When the line intersect horizontal plane that's called.....

a] horizontal trace

b] vertical trace

c] trace of line

d] none of these

74]Planes may be divided into two main types ......

a] Perpendicular planes, auxillary planes

b] Perpendicular plane, oblique planes

c] Auxillary planes , perpendicular planes

d] none of these

75] Planes which are inclined to the reference plane are called......

a] Auxillary plane
b] obliqeu plane
c] Perpendicular planes
d] picture plane

76] When a plane is perpendicular to a reference plane it's projection on that plane is a..........

a] horizontal line
b] parallel line
c] straight line
d] none of these

77] When a plane is parallel to a reference plane , it's projection on that plane shows........

a] It's true shape &size
b] It's true length & size
c] It's true height & size
d] none of these

78] Plane perpendicular to VP & HP that plane is called as ....

a] Auxillary Plane
b] Oblique Plane
c] Perpendicular Plane
d] None of these

79] Perpendicular plane can be divides into the following types.........

a] Perpendicular to both the reference planes.
b] Perpendicular to one plane & parallel to other
c] Perpendicular to one plane & inclined to other
d] All of these

80] The planes have only two dimensions, viz........

a] Length & breadth
b] Length & height
c] Length & thickness
d] All of these

81] The imaginary line of prism joining the centrs of the bases called.........

a] Faces
b] Axis
c] Apex
d] Base

82] A right & regular prism has it's axis....... to the bases

a] Parallel
b] Perpendicular
c] Inclined
d] None of these

83] When a pyramid or a cone is cut by a plane parallel to it's base thus removing the top portion, the remaining portion is called it's.........

a] Sphere
b] Cone
c] Cylinder
d] Frustum

84] Oblique cylinder & cones have their axes........ to their base

a] Inclined
b] Parallel
c] Perpendicular
d] All of these

85] Projection of two equal sphere s resting on the ground & in contact with each other, with the line joining there centre parallel to the..........

a] A VP
b] VP
c] HP
d] All of these

86] Projections of section on the other plane to which it is inclined is called.......

a] Section planes
b] Apparent section
c] True shape of sphere
d] None of these

87] When the section plane is parallel to the HP or the ground, the true shape of the section will be seen in.........

a] Front view
b] Side view
c] Top view
d] All of these

88] Surface of solid are laid out on a plane the figure obtained is called its........

a] Interpenetration
b] Development
c] Intersection

d] None of these

89] Development of surfaces is essential in.........

a] Foundry shop

b] <u>Sheet metal work</u>

c] Fitting shop

d] None of these

90] Which method of development used in transition pieces?

a] Parallel diameter

b] Radial line method

c] <u>Triangulation method</u>

d] Approximate method

91] Which method of development used in pyramids and cones.........

a] <u>Radial line method</u>

b] Parallel line method

c] Approximate method

d] Triangulation method

92] Parallel line method is used in..........

a] Prism

b] Cylinder

c] Cubes

d] <u>All of these</u>

93] Which method of development used in surface as sphere, paraboloid, ellipsoid, hyperboloid, and helicoids

a] Radial line method

b] Triangulation method

c] <u>Approximate method</u>

d] Parallel line method

94] Zone method and lune method is used in development of........

a] Prisms

b] Cones

c] <u>Sphere</u>

d] Pyramids

95] Calculation the subtended angle Θ by the formula $\Theta = 360^0 \times$ radius of the base circle

a] <u>Length of axis</u>

b] <u>Slant height</u>

c] Radius of axis

d] None of these

96] In engineering practice, objects constructed may have constituent part, the surfaces of which intersect one another in lines called........ of intersection.

a] Lines

b] Cones

c] Cylinder

d] Prisms

97] The line of interaction may be depending upon the nature of.......

a] Intersection surface

b] Intersecting solids

c] Intersection cones

d] None of these

98] The two plane surface intersect in a........ line

a] Curve

b] Straight

c] Plane

d] All of these

99] The line of intersection between two curved surface or between......... Surface and a curved surface is a curve.

a] A curved

b] A plane

c] A solids

d] None of these

100] When a solids completely penetration another solids there will be two lines of intersection. These lines are sometimes called the line or........

a] Line of interpenetration

b] Curve of interpenetration

c] Solids of interpenetration

d] All of these

101] Use of penetration curve is.......

a] Sheet metal work

b] Fitting shop

c] Fabricating work

d] Foundry shop

102] Methods of dctermining the line of intersection between surface of two interpenetration.........

a] Approximate method & radial line method

b] Line method and cutting plane method

c] Triangulation method and parallel line method

d] None of these

103] Example of interpenetration is..........

a] Two prism intersection

b] Cylinder and prism intersection

c] Cone and cylinders intersection

d] <u>All of these</u>

104] Two cylinder intersection is example of.........

a] <u>Intersection</u>

b] Interpenetration

c] Cone intersection

d] None of these

105] .... Method is explained in detail while solving illustrative problems

a] Line method

b] Radial line method

c] <u>Cutting plane method</u>

d] Parallel line method

106] What is a type of isometric projection?

a] <u>Pictorial projection</u>

b] Orthographic projection

c] Perspective projection

d] Oblique Projection

107] Isometric views have been drawn........

a] Full scale

b] Half scale

c] <u>True length</u>

d] True scale

108] The line parallel to isometric axis are called........

a] Isometric axis

b] <u>Isometric line</u>

c] Isometric planes

d] Isometric views

109] The isometric projection is reduce in the ratio.........

a] 3 :

b] 1 : 2

c] 2 : 2

d] <u>2 : 3</u>

110] The isometric projection of circle drawn with........
a] Isometric Plane
b] Isometric graph
c] Isometric Drawing
d] <u>Isometric Scale</u>
111] The major axis of the ellipse is long than..............
a] Radius of the circle
b] True diameter
c] <u>Diameter of the circle</u>
d] None of these
112] Makes practice for drawing of isometric view using........
a] Isometric planes
b] Isometric lines
c] <u>Isometric graph</u>
d] Isometric view
113] Use of parabolic curve is
a] <u>Sound reflectors</u>
b] Dams
c] Man hole of boiler
d] Gland & stuffing box
114] When the section plane is inclined the true shape of section on
a] AVP
b] VP
c] HP
d] <u>A/P</u>
115] When section plane is perpendicular to both the HP & VP the true shape of section on
a]Top view
b] <u>Side view</u>
c] Front view
d]None of this
116] When view projected on auxiliary planes are called
a] <u>Auxiliary view</u>
b Sectional view
c] Front view
d] None of these
117] Invisible features of an object are shown by means of
a] Outline

b] Chain lines
c] Hidden lines
d] None of these

118] Importance of sectional view on drawing for
a] Internal details
b] Outer details
c] Hatching
d] None of these

119] The component is cut by a straight cutting plane is divided in to two parts
a] Half section
b] Full section
c] Offset section
d] Removed section

120] section line is two different parts (pieces] in contact should be drown in...
a] Same direction
b] Opposite direction
c]parallel direction
d] None of these

121] When area to be sectioned in very small as for this plate and structural members blacked in section may be used. A space of not less than
a] 0.07mm
b] 0.7mm
c] 0.05mm
d] 0.5mm

122] The sum of interior angles of polygon is equal
a] (2*n-4]*Right angle
b] (2*n]*Right angle-4
c] (2*4-n]*Right angle
d] (2-4*n]*Right angle

123] One micron is equal to ....mm
a] 0.001
b] 1000
c] 0.01
d] 0.1

124] Development of surface is essential in.....
a] foundry shop

b] sheet metal work
c] fitting shop
d] none of these
125] Which method of development used in transition piece?
a] parallel line method
b] radial line method
c] triangulation method
d] none of these
126] The isometric projection is reduced in the ratio of
a] √2:√3
b] √3:√2
c] 1:√2
d] none of these
127] When measurements are required in three units the scale is used....
a] full scale
b] plain scale
c] half scale
d] none of these
128]Isometric drawing is larger in production about isometric projection is....
a] 22.5%
b] 0.815
c] 9/11
d] none of these
129] While isometric of sphere of spherical parts.......is must be used.
a] full scale
b] isometric length
c] true length
d] half scale
130] When circle draw with isometric scale the length of major axis of the ellipse to the ....
a] true diameter
b] isometric diameter
c] isometric diameter
d] none of these
131] In isometric view which contain a large number of non –isometric lines which method is used
a] box method

b] off-set method
c] co-ordinate method
d] centre lay out method

132] When drawing is drawn smaller than actual size of object .....
a] full scale
b] enlarging scale
c] reducing scale
d] none of these

133] When e=1 curve is called.....
a] parabola
b] hyperbola
c] ellipse
d] none of these

134]Compare with isometric drawing the advantage of oblique projection is....
a] front face is in true shape
b] two axis are always perpendicular to each othe
c] receding axis is taken at some convenient angles
d] none of these

135]If all the receding edges are drawn true length the oblique projection is called...
a] cavilier projection
b] cabinet projection
c] general projection
d] none of these

136] The large object such as building the point is usually taken height of .....
a] 0.8mm
b] 1.2mm
c] 1.8mm
d] 1.5mm

137] Central plane is the imaginary vertical plane which passes through....
a] P. P
b] H.L
c] G.P
d] C.P

138] When object is parallel to P.P the perspective is called......

a] one point
b] two point
c] three point
d] none of these
139] The line drawn through the station point from the picture plane shall be ....
a] P.A
b] H.L
c] G.L
d] C
140] The distance of the station point from the picture plane shall be .....
a] Max. Diameter of the object
b] Twice the max. Diameter of the object
c] Half the max. Diameter of the object
d] none of these
141] In isometric view of hexagonal plane all the sides of hexagon is .....
a] equal length
b] unequal length
c] none of these
142] When all the faces are equal & regular the polyhedron is said....
a] regular
b] prisms
c] irregular
d] pyramid
143] Oblique prisms &pyramid have ......
a] axis perpendicular to the base
b] axis inclined to the base
c] faces inclined to the H.P
d] none of these
144] Icosahedrons has equal equilateral triangular faces
a] 12
b] 8
c] 20
d] 6
145] When a pyramid or cone is cut by a plane parallel to its base is called.....
a] pyramid
b] turned carted

c] frustum

d] none of these

146] Plane which are inclined to both the reference plane is called ......

a] oblique plane

b] perpendicular plane

c] inclined plane

d] none of these

147] When a line parallel to H.P & perpendicular to V.P the trace line is.....

a] V.T

b] H.T

c] no trace

d] V.T& H.T

148] When a line parallel to the V.P and inclined to H.P the true length of line in.....

a] front view

b] top view

c] side view

d] none of these

149] When point situated in front quadrant

a] above the H.P & in front of V.P

b] below the H.P & in front of V.P

c] behind the V.P & above H.P

d] below the H.P & behind the V.P

150] Find the quadrant of point "b" is 15 mm above H.P and 25mm behind the V.P

a] I st

b] III rd

c] IIII th

d] II nd

151] In first angle projection front view is ......

a] above the top view

b] below the top view

c] above the side view

d] below the side view

152] In orthographic projection the projectors are ....

a] parallel to plane

b] perpendicular to plane

c] inclined to plane

d] none of these

153] L.H.S.V means.........

a] length of side view

b] left hand view

c] right hand view

d] left hand side view

154] The object lines between the observer and the plane of projection is ....

a] 3rd angle

b] 1st angle

c] 4th angle

d] 2nd angle

155] In third angle projection plane of projection is assumed to be ......

a] non transparent

b] quadrant

c] transparent

d] dihedral angle

156] In third angle projection top view is always on......

a] above front view

b] above top view

c] below the front view

d] below the side view

157] Four quadrants which may be called as......

a] anticlockwise

b] first and third angle

c] dihedral angles

d] none of these

158] In first angle projection method the view see from the left is placed on .....

a] left of the front view

b] right of front view

c] above the top view

d] below the front view

159] The size of A2 paper is .....

a] 297*420

b] 594*841

c] 420*594

d] 210*297

160] The edge of board on which 'T' square is sli9ding is called ......

a] straight edge

b] working edge

c] chisel edge

d] none of these

161] The size of title block as recommended by B.I.S . is .....

a] 185*65

b] 150*50

c] 170*65

d] none of these

162] For A2 size sheet the number of zones suggested by B.I.S. along the length & width.......

a] 12,8

b] 16,12

c] 8,6

d] none of these

163] The drawing sheet is so folded that...... is always on the top.

a] drawing

b] lettering

c] title block

d] none of these

164] In free hand sketching horizontal lines are sketched from.......

a] right to left

b] up to down

c] left to right

d] none of these

165] When drawing is down smaller than actual size of object

a] enlarging scale

b] reducing scale

c] full scale

d] none of these

166] The ratio of the length of the object represented on drawing to the actual length of object is called.......

a] full scale

b] R.F.

c] half scale

d] plain scale

167] When measurements are required in three unit the scale is used.....
a] full scale
b] half scale
c] plain scale
d] none of these
168] When protractor is not available the scale of chord is used ......
a] measure length
b] measure angle
c] measure scale
d] none of these
169] The least count of a vernier calliper is ....
a] 0.001
b] 0.02
c] 0.001
d] 0.0002
170] Which scale is used to read a very small unit with great accuracy?
a] plain scale
b] diagonal scale
c] scale of chord
d] vernier scale
171] The R.F. is greater than one (1] the scale is ....
a] plain scale
b] diagonal scale
c] enlarging scale
d] reducing scale

Electrical MCQ for Aeronautical Engineering

85] A heater draws a current of 8A when connected to a 240V source] What is the resistance value of the heater element in ohms?
A] 40
B] 20
C] 30
D] 60
86] An electric soldering iron with an 80 ohms heating element is plugged into a 240V outlet] How much current will be drawn by the iron?
A] 2A
B] 3A
C] 4A
D] 5A

87] The alternator in a car delivers 4A and has a load of 3 ohms connected across its terminals] Find the voltage of the circuit

A] 18V

B] 24V

C] 12V

D] 16V

88] Three resistors of 1K ohms, 2K ohms and 7K ohms are connected in series with a 30 V supply] If 2 K ohms and 7 K ohms resistors are open circuited, a voltmeter connected across the 7K ohms resistor will indicate...

A] 10 k ohms, 3A

B] 10 k ohms, 300mA

C] 10 k ohms, 3 mA

D] 5 k ohms, 6 mA

89] A voltage source produces an IR drop of 40V across a 20 ohms resistance, 60V across a 30 ohms resistance and 180V across a 90 ohms resistance all in series] How much is the applied voltage?

A] 180 V

B] 240 V

C] 100 V

D] 280 V

90] Three resistors 27 ohms, 47 ohms and 68 ohms are connected in parallel] What is the otal resistance?

A] less than 27 ohms

B] greater than 68 ohms

C] between 27 and 47 ohms

D] sum of all the three resistances

91] One million and one mege ohms resistors are there if connected both in parallel, what would be the combined resistance value?

A] 0.5 mega ohm

B] 0.5 milli ohm

C] 0.5 kilo ohm

D] 0.5 ohm

92] A 24 ohms and a 8 ohms resistors in parallel gets a combined resistance of...

A] 6 ohms

B] 12 ohms

C] 3 ohms

D] 32 ohms

93] Resistors of the following values are connected in parallel, 5 ohms, 5 kilo-ohms, 50 kilo-ohms, 5 mega ohms] Their equivalent resistance will be very near to...

A] 4.5 ohms

B] 4500 ohms

C] 45000 ohms

D] 4,500,000 ohms

94] The resistance of given wire is 2 ohms] The resistance of the other wire made of the same material having twice the length and twice the cross sectional area is...

A] 5 ohms

B] 6 ohms

C] 2 ohms

D] 8 ohms

95] If the area of a metal wire of a given length is doubles, its resistance will...

A] be doubled

B] be halved

C] remain the same

D] be four times more

96].Among the following only one is regarded as resistance wire

A] gold

B] silver

C] nichrome

D] copper

97] Arc heating occurs when the air between electrodes of opposite polarity becomes..

A] moistened

B] dry

C] ionized

D] none of the above

98] The meter used to measure the temperature of furnace is...

A] hydrometer

B] pyrometer

C] hygrometer

D] tachometer

99] in the case of electrolyte a rise in temperature causes...

A] decrease in resistance

B] increase in resistance

C] no change in resistance

D] none of the above

100] Heat developed in a conductor is proportional to the...

A] square of the power

B] square of the resistance

C] square of the current

D] square of the time

101] Out of the four metal/alloys given below, one has almost no change in resistance for temperature change...

A] nickel

B] nichrome

C] platinum

D] manganin

102] A material that is slightly repelled by a magnet is called ...

A] magnetic

B] paramagnetic

C] diamagnetic

D] ferromagnetic

103] A material that can be magnetized only very slightly is called...

A] magnetic

B] paramagnetic

C] diamagnetic

D] ferromagnetic

104] Substances that can be magnetized easily and make very strong magnets are called...

A] ferromagnetic

B] diamagnetic

C] paramagnetic

D] permanent magnetic

105] A substance that has a high retentivity can be used for the manufacture of...

A] electromagnets

B] permanent magnets

C] temporary magnets

D] paramagnets

106] A substance that has low retentivity can be used for the manufacture of...

A] electromagnets
B] permanent magnets
C] bar magnets
D] paramagnets
107] The symbol for inductance is...
A] H
B] I
C] L
D] X
108] Tube lamp choke is the best example of...
A] open circuited
B] short circuited
C] grounded
D] connected to the neutral line
109] The initial function of a choke in a tube light circuit is to...
A] limit the starting current
B] induce high voltage
C] heat up the filament
D] limit the current after starting
110] The second function of a choke in a tube light circuit is to...
A] limit the starting current
B] induce high voltage
C] heat up the filament
D] limit the current after starting
111] The periodic time of a wave from is 2ms] Calculate the frequency
A] 50 HZ
B] 5 HZ
C] 500HZ
D] 5 KHZ
112] How big is the peak amplitude of a sine-wave with an effective value of 220 volts?
A] 311 V
B] 380 V
C] 400 V
D] 440 V
113] The peak-to-peak voltage is 99V] how big is the effective value of the sine wave?
A] 70 V

B] 44.5V
C] 49.5 V
D] 35 V

114] A moving coil voltmeter reads 10 V AC] How big is the effective voltage?

A] higher
B] lower
C] the same
D] 10% higher

115] A moving iron ammeter reads 10 A] how big is the peak current of the oscillation?

A] 7.07 A
B] 1.1414A
C] 70.7 A
D] 14.1 A

116] A current of 2 amps flows through a resistance of 10 ohms] The power dissipated in the resistance is equal to...

A] 20 watts
B] 200 watts
C] 40 watts
D] 5 watts

117] If the frequency changes from 50 HZ to 100 HZ keeping voltage constant, the inductive reactance of coil connected to supply...

A] remains same
B] become half
C] become doubled
D] become 4 times

118] Capacitance is not affected by...

A] plate area
B] distance between plates
C] dialectic material
D] frequency

119] The capacitive reactance of a capacitor varies...

A] directly with frequency
B] inversely with frequency
C] directly with applied voltage
D] inversely with applied voltage

120] A capacitor acquired 3 coulombs of charge when 6 volts are applied across it] It has a capacitance of ...

A] 0.5 farad

B] 3 farads

C] 3 farads

D] 18 farads

121] A capacitor is connected across a 200 volt AC line, its minimum voltage rating should be...

A] 100 volts

B] 200 Volts

C] 300 volts

D] 400 volts

122] when testing a capacitor with an ohmmeter, the meter indicates some resistance] The capacitor under test is...

A] leaky

B] open

C] good

D] short

123] The total capacitance of a 40 micro farad capacitor connected in series with an 80 micro farad capacitor is...

A] 26.7 micro farad

B] 40 micro farad

C] 60.6 micro farad

D] 120 micro farad

124] For obtaining 1 micro farad capacitor from 3 nos] of 3 micro farad capacitors we have to connect...

A] all in parallel

B] all in series

C] 2 series and one in parallel

D] none of the above

125] In an AC series circuit having R and C the current flowing through the capacitor will be...

A] lagging the voltage

B] leading the voltage

C] in phase with the voltage

D] none of the above

126] If the frequency of the supply is increased in the R-C series circuit the capacitive reactance will be

A] reduced
B] increased
C] having no effect
D] none of the above

127] Power companies are interested in improving the power factor to
A] reduce line current
B] increase motor efficiency
C] increase volt-amperes
D] decrease power

128] A capacitor increases the power factor value of an AC motor load when it is connected...
A] in series with the motor
B] in series with the starter
C] in parallel with the motor
D] in series with the main winding

129] Normally, the power factor of an incandescent lighting circuit is..
A] 0
B] 0.5
C] 0.707
D] 1.0

130] When resistance alone is used to determine current in an RLC series circuit, the circuit is...
A] an inductive circuit
B] a capacitive circuit
C] a combination circuit
D] a resonant circuit

131] Inductive reactance is directly related to..
A] resistance
B] frequency
C] capacitance
D] power

132] Synchronous motor when used for power factor improvement should be...
A] under excited
B] over excited
C] loaded
D] running at no load

133] In a RL parallel circuit, the opposition to total current is called...

A] reactance
B] resistance
C] a vector sum
D] impedance
134] In a AC parallel RL circuit, the power dissipated at the
A] impedance
B] resistance
C] inductance
D] capacitance
135] How much is the nominal output voltage of a carbon zinc cell?
A] 12V
B] 1.5V
C] 2.0V
D] 2.2V
136] Cells are connected in series to..
A] increase the output voltage
B] decreases the output voltage
C] decrease the internal resistance
D] increase the current capacity
54137connected in
A] series
B] parallel
C] series-parallel
D] parallel-series
138] The capacity of a cell is measured in
A] watt-hour
B] watts
C] amperes
D] ampere-hour
139] The primary cell which has the shortest shelf life is
A] carbon – zinc
B] alkaline
C] mercury
D] lithium
140] The cell which has very high energy density for given weight or volume to
A] carbon-zinc
B] alkaline

C] mercury
D] lithium
141] A 100-Ah capacity battery should deliver a current of 8A for approximately...
A] 12 h
B] 8 h
C] 20 h
D] 100 h
142] When the battery is needed to be kept idle for a long time...
A] overcharge the battery
B] remove electrolyte
C] clean the plates with distilled water
D] dry them and store the battery in cool dry clean place
143] The active materials of the nickel iron cell are...
A] nickel hydroxide
B] powdered iron and its oxide
C] 21% solution of caustic potash
D] all the above materials
144] The capacity of a cell is measured in
A] watt hour
B] watts
C] amperes
D] ampere-hour
145] To charge a secondary cell, the system used is
A] low voltage AC
B] high voltage AC
C] AC
D] DC
146] What is the number of phases in a normal industrial supply system?
A] one
B] three
C] four
D] two
147] In a 3 phase star connected alternator, the coils have a phase difference of...
A] 120◦
B] 240◦
C] 60◦

D] 360◦

148] Delta connection is used no one of the following

A] primary of the transmission line transformer

B] alternator winding

C] secondary of the distribution transformer

D] primary of the distribution transformer

149] Which method can be used to measure the power in a 3-phase unbalanced load system?

A] one wattmeter method

B] tow wattmeter method

C] three wattmeter method

D] three ammeter method

150] Two wattmeters can be used to measure 3-hase power in a 3-phase, 3 wire system with...

A] balanced load

B] unbalanced load

C] balanced as well as unbalanced load

D] out of balanced load

151] A single wattmeter can be used to measure power in a 3-phase system only when the load is..

A] balanaced

B] unbalanced

C] balanced as well as unbalanced load

D] constant

152] The force producing movement of the pointer in an indicating instrument is called as...

A] deflecting force

B] controlling force

C] damping force

D] distracting force

153] A permanent magnet moving coil instrument will read...

A] only AC quantities

B] only DC quantities

C] both AC and DC quantities

D] pulsating quantities

154] An instrument using gravity control will read correctly if used in..

A] vertical position only

B] horizontal position only

C] inclined position only

D] any position

155] Which one of the following damping methods is used in permanent magnet moving coil instrument?

A] air damping

B] fluid damping

C] spring damping

D] eddy current damping

156] Moving coil instrument works on the effect of...

A] chemical effect

B] heating effect

C] electrostatic effect

D] electromagnetic effect

157] The meter installed at your house to measure electrical energy is an example of...

A] indication type instrument

B] recording type instrument

C] indicating as well as recording type instrument

D] integrating type instrument

158].Which of the following material is preferred for permanent magnet?

A] alnico

B] y-alloy

C] silicon steel

D] wrought iron

159] The instrument which could be classified as absolute instrument is...

A] milli ammeter

B] micro ammeter

C] galvanometer

D] tangent galvanomer

160] Which of the following methods of damping is commonly used in moving iron instrument?

A] Air damping

B] fluid damping

C] eddy current damping

D] viscosity damping

161] The deflecting torque of a moving iron instrument is directly proportional to the..

A] current

B] square of the current

C] square root of the current

D] voltage

162]Which of the following is used for measuring the medium resistance directly?

A] ammeter

B] megger

C] ohmmeter

D] voltmeter

163] An ohmmeter is used for measuring the...

A] insulation resistance

B] resistance

C] current

D] potential difference

164] Which of the following components is not a part of an ohmmeter?

A] fixed resistor

B] variable resistor

C] capacitor

D] battery

165] In shunt ohmmeter, maximum deflection signifies ..

A] maximum resistance

B] minimum resistance

C] a fault in the megger

D] none of these

166].An unknown DC voltage is to be measured, which measuring range will you select first?

A] 500V

B] 50V

C] 1.5 V

D] 0.5V

167].An unknown direct current of micro ampere rating is to be measured, which measuring range will you select first?

A] 20 micro amp

B] 15 micro amp

C] 150 micro amp

D] 500 micro amp

168] A multimeter cannot measure...

A] current

B] potential difference

C] capacitance

D] resistance

169] Dynamometer type meters are used to measure...

A] only AC quantities

B] only DC quantities

C] both AC and DC

D] pulsating AC only

170] Which effect is used in wattmeter?

A] electrodynamic effect

B] thermal effect

C] chemical effect

D] electrostatic effect

171] Which of the instrument listed below operates efficiently as wattmeter in both AC and DC?

A] PMMC instrument

B] dynamometer instrument

C] hot wire instrument

D] MI instrument

172] Electrodynamic type of instrument are used commonly for the measurement of...

A] voltage

B] current

C] resistance D]

173] When the phase and neutral of the energy meter are interchanged, its disc...

A] rotates in reverse direction

B] rotates in correct direction

C] will stop

D] rotates slowly

E] rotates at high speed

174] When the disc of energy meter is rotating even without connecting any load, the error is called

A] creeping error

B] phase error

C] friction error

D] temperature error

175] AC single phase energy meters record the energy in the unit of...

A] kilowatt hours

B] number of thousands of disc rotation

C] volt amperes

D] kilo volt ampere

176] A megger measures resistance in...

A] ohms

B] hundreds of ohms

C] thousands of ohms

D] millions of ohms

177] A megger is exclusively designed for measuring..

A] very high resistance

B] very low resistance

C] ground faults in power lines

D] over loads on DC motors

178] For pipe earthing the minimum internal diameter of galvanized iron of steel pipe required is...

A] 12.5 mm

B] 16mm

C] 3.5 mm

D] 4 m

179] The earth conductor provides a path to ground for..

A] leakage current

B] over current

C] high voltage

D] circuit current

180] if the size of the circuit copper conductor is 10 sq-mm then the size of earth conductor in G.I] wire should be...

A] 1.5 sq.mm

B] 2.5 sq.mm

C] 5 sq.mm

D] 10 sq.mm

181] One calory is equal to,,,

A] 4187 joules

B] 418.7 joules

C] 41.87 joules

D] 4.187 joules

182] The operating temperature range of electrical stove with bare heating element is...

A] 300◦ to 400◦C

B] 500◦ to 600◦C

C] 550◦ to 900◦C

D] 1100◦ to 1300◦C

183] Which appliance works on heating effect of electric current?

A] incandescent lamp

B] bimetallic thermostat

C] H R C fuse

D] toaster

184] What is the size of nichrome wire for heating element of 1000 watts, 230V heater at 500◦C?

A] 18 SWG

B] 20SWG

C] 24 SWG

D] 25 SWG

185] The heat proof insulating material used for heater base is...

A] mica

B] porcelain

C] asbestos

D] glass wool

186].The temperature regulating component of an automatic electric iron is...

A] heating element

B] thermostat

C] sole plate

D] pressure plate

187].The bread toasting zone temperature is about...

A] 400◦C

B] 800◦C

C] 260◦C

D] 975◦C

188] If a winding makes electrical contact with the metal case of the mixer motor the winding is...

A] grounded

B] open circuited
C] short circuited
D] loose connected
189] If the end shafts of a rotor turns blue it is an indication of...
A] scoring
B] overheating
C] freezing
D] burring
190] What type of motor is used in a food mixer?
A] DC shunt motor
B] universal motor
C] capacitor start motor
D] capacitor start and run motor
191] In what position is the motor mounted in most of the mixers?
A] vertical
B] horizontal
C] inclined
D] parallel

Fluid Mechanics for Aeronautical Engineering

1. Which one is in a state of failure?
a) Solid
b) Liquid
c) Gas
d) Fluid

2. A small shear force is applied on an element and then removed. If the element regains it's original position, what kind of an element can it be?
a) Solid
b) Liquid
c) Fluid
d) Gaseous

3. In which type of matter, one won't find a free surface?
a) Solid
b) Liquid
c) Gas
d) Fluid

4. If a person studies about a fluid which is at rest, what will you call his domain of study?
a) Fluid Mechanics

b) Fluid Statics
c) Fluid Kinematics
d) Fluid Dynamics

5. The value of the compressibility of an ideal fluid is
a) zero
b) unity
c) infinity
d) more than that of a real fluid

6. The value of the Bulk Modulus of an ideal fluid is
a) zero
b) unity
c) infinity
d) less than that of a real fluid

7. The value of the viscosity of an ideal fluid is
a) zero
b) unity
c) infinity
d) more than that of a real fluid

8. The value of the surface tension of an ideal fluid is
a) zero
b) unity
c) infinity
d) more than that of a real fluid

8. Which of the following statement is true about vapor pressure of a liquid?

a) Vapor pressure is closely related to molecular activity and temperature of the liquid

b) Vapor pressure is closely related to molecular activity but independent of the temperature of the liquid

c) Vapor pressure is not affected by molecular activity and temperature of the liquid

d) Vapor pressure is not affected by molecular activity and is independent of the temperature of the liquid

9. Which of the following equation correctly depicts the relation between the vapor pressure of a liquid and it's temperature?

a) Vapor pressure increases linearly with the increase in temperature of the liquid

b) Vapor pressure increases slightly with the increase in temperature of the liquid at low temperatures and the rate of increase goes high at higher temperatures

c) Vapor pressure increases rapidly with the increase in temperature of the liquid at low temperatures and the rate of increase goes low at higher temperatures

d) Vapor pressure remains unchanged with the increase in temperature of the liquid

10. Which of the following is the condition for the boiling of a liquid?

a) Absolute pressure of a liquid must be greater than or equal to it's vapor pressure

b) Absolute pressure of a liquid must be less than or equal to it's vapor pressure

c) Absolute pressure of a liquid must be equal to it's vapor pressure

d) Absolute pressure of a liquid must be greater than it's vapor pressure

11. Which of the following machines have the possibility of cavitation?

a) Reaction turbines and centrifugal pumps

b) Reaction turbines and reciprocating pumps

c) Impulse turbines and centrifugal pumps

d) Impulse turbines and reciprocating pumps

12. The three liquids 1, 2, and 3 with vapor pressures V1, V2 and V3 respectively, are kept under same pressure. If V1 > V2 > V3, which liquid will start boiling early?

a) liquid 1

b) liquid 2

c) liquid 3

d) they will start boiling at the same time

13. Equal amount of a particular liquid is poured into three similar containers, namely 1, 2 and 3, at a temperature of T1, T2 and T3 respectively. If T1 < T2 < T3, the liquid in which container will have the highest vapor pressure?

a) container 1

b) container 2

c) container 3

d) the vapor pressure of the liquid will remain the same irrespective of it's temperature

14. The absolute pressure of a water is 0.5kN above it's vapor pressure. If it flows with a velocity of 1m/s, what will be the value of Cavitation

Number describing the flow induced boiling?

a) 0.25

b) 0.5

c) 1

d) 2

15. Which of the following is correct regarding the formation and collapse of vapor bubbles in a liquid?

a) Vapor bubbles are formed when the fluid pressure goes above the vapor pressure and collapses when the fluid pressure goes above the bubble pressure

b) Vapor bubbles are formed when the fluid pressure goes above the vapor pressure and collapses when the fluid pressure goes below the bubble pressure

c) Vapor bubbles are formed when the fluid pressure drops below the vapor pressure and collapses when the fluid pressure goes below the bubble pressure

d) Vapor bubbles are formed when the fluid pressure drops below the vapor pressure and collapses when the fluid pressure goes above the bubble pressure

Pneumatics for Aeronautical Engineering

1. Fluid power circuits use schematic drawings to:

a) Simplify component function details

b) Make it so only trained persons can understand the functions

c) Make the drawing look impressive

d) Make untrained person to understand

2. A pneumatic symbol is:

a) Different from a hydraulic symbol used for the same function

b) The same as a hydraulic symbol used for the same function

c) Not to be compared to a hydraulic symbol used for the same function

d) None of the mentioned

3. Pneumatic systems usually do not exceed:

a) 1 hp

b) 1 to 2 hp

c) 2 to 3 hp

d) 4 to 5 hp

4. Most hydraulic circuits:

a) Operate from a central hydraulic power unit

b) Use air-over-oil power units

c) Have a dedicated power unit
d) Does not have dedicated power unit
5. Hydraulic and pneumatic circuits:
a) Perform the same way for all functions
b) Perform differently for all functions
c) Perform the same with some exceptions
d) Does not perform all the functions
6. The lubricator in a pneumatic circuit is the:
a) First element in line
b) Second element in line
c) Last element in line
d) Third element in line
7. When comparing first cost of hydraulic systems to pneumatic systems, generally they are:
a) More expensive to purchase
b) Less expensive to purchase
c) Cost is same
d) Cost is not required
8. When comparing operating cost of hydraulic systems to pneumatic systems, generally they are.
a) More expensive to operate
b) Less expensive to operate
c) Cost is same to operate
d) Cost is not required
9. The most common hydraulic fluid is:
a) Mineral oil
b) Synthetic fluid
c) Water
d) Gel

Instrumentation System in Aeronautical Engineering

1. Beer Lambert's law gives the relation between which of the following?
a) Reflected radiation and concentration
b) Scattered radiation and concentration
c) Energy absorption and concentration
d) Energy absorption and reflected radiation
2. In which of the following ways, absorption is related to transmittance?
a) Absorption is the logarithm of transmittance
b) Absorption is the reciprocal of transmittance

c) Absorption is the negative logarithm of transmittance

d) Absorption is a multiple of transmittance

3. Which of the following is not a limitation of Beer Lambert's law, which gives the relation between absorption, thickness and concentration?

a) Concentration must be lower

b) Radiation must have higher bandwidth

c) Radiation source must be monochromatic

d) Does not consider factors other than thickness and concentration that affect absorbance

4. Beer's law states that the intensity of light decreases with respect to ____________

a) Concentration

b) Distance

c) Composition

d) Volume

5. Lambert's law states that the intensity of light decreases with respect to ____________

a) Concentration

b) Distance

c) Composition

d) Volume

6. The representation of Beer Lambert's law is given as A = abc. If 'b' represents distance, 'c' represents concentration and 'A' represents absorption, what does 'a' represent?

a) Intensity

b) Transmittance

c) Absorptivity

d) Admittance

7. Which of the following is not true about Absorption spectroscopy?

a) It involves transmission

b) Scattering is kept minimum

c) Reflection is kept maximum

d) Intensity of radiation leaving the substance is an indication of concentration

8. Transmittance is given as T = P/Po. If Po is the power incident on the sample, what does P represent?

a) Radiant power transmitted by the sample

b) Radiant power absorbed by the sample

c) Sum of powers absorbed and scattered

d) Sum of powers transmitted and reflected

9. What is the unit of absorbance which can be derived from Beer Lambert's law?

a) L mol-1 cm-1

b) L gm-1 cm-1

c) Cm

d) No unit

10. What is the unit of molar absorptivity or absorptivity which is used to determine absorbance A in Beer Lambert's formula?

a) L mol-1 cm-1

b) L gm-1 cm-1

c) Cm

d) No unit

11. Which of the following is not a source used in Mid Infrared Spectrophotometer?

a) Nernst glower

b) High pressure mercury arc lamp

c) Globar

d) Nichrome wire

12. Which of the following is the wave number of near infrared spectrometer?

a) 4000 – 200 cm-1

b) 200 – 10 cm-1

c) 12500 – 4000 cm-1

d) 50 – 1000 cm-1

13. Which of the following options are correct in terms of wavelength for the different types of IR spectrometer?

a) Near IR: 0.8 – 2.5 mm

b) Mid IR: 0.8 – 2.5 mm

c) Far IR: 2.5 – 50 mm

d) Mid IR: 50 – 100 mm

14. Which of the following is not a composition of Nernst glower or Nernst filament?

a) Oxidcs of Zirconium

b) Oxides of Barium

c) Oxides of Yitrium

d) Oxides of Thorium

15. What is the composition of Globar rod which is used as a source in Mid IR spectroscopy?

a) Silicon carbide

b) Silver chloride

c) Silicon dioxide

d) Silver carbide

16. Bolometer, a type of detector, is also known as:

a) Resistance temperature detector (RTD)

b) Thermistor

c) Thermocouple

d) Golay cell

17. Which of the following is not a technique for preparing solid samples in IR spectroscopy?

a) Solids run in solution

b) Mull technique

c) Solid films

d) Thin films

18. Which of the following is not used as pyroelectric material used in pyroelectric transducers in Infrared spectroscopy?

a) Triglycine Sulphate

b) Deutrated Triglycine Sulphate

c) Some Polymers

d) Tetraglycine sulphate

19. Which of the following is the principle of Golay cell which is used as a detector in IR spectroscopy?

a) Expansion of gas upon heating

b) Increase in resistance due to increase in temperature and vice versa

c) Temperature difference gives rise to a potential difference in the material

d) Decrease in resistance due to increase in temperature

20. In a solid sample treatment technique, the finely ground solid sample is mixed with mineral oil to make a thick paste which is then spread between IR transmitting windows. What is the name of this solid sample treatment technique?

a) Pressed pellet

b) Mull technique

c) Solid films

d) Solids run in solution

Manufacturing Technology in Aeronautical Engineering

1. Which of the following have a non-crystalline structure?

a) Iron

b) Quartz

c) Silica glass

d) Tungsten

2. Which of the following have a non-crystalline structure?

a) Steel

b) Nickel

c) High density polythene

d) Low density polythene

3. Which of the following is a characteristic of crystalline structure?

a) High density

b) Low density

c) Range of melting point

d) Varying structure

4. Which of the following is characteristic of non-crystalline structures?

a) Long range of periodicity

b) Well defined structure and geometry

c) Low density

d) Sharp diffraction pattern

5. Which of the following factor is not responsible for the formation of a non-crystalline structure?

a) Atomic packing has open structure

b) Primary bonds are absent

c) Formation of 1-dimensional chain molecule

d) Strong secondary bond

6. A cubic unit cell satisfies which of the following equations?

a) $a=b=c, \alpha=\beta=\Upsilon=90$ degree

b) $a \neq b=c, \alpha=\beta=\Upsilon=90$ degree

c) $a=b \neq c, \alpha=\beta=\Upsilon=90$ degree

d) $a=b=c, \alpha \neq \beta=\Upsilon=90$ degree

7. A tetragon unit cell satisfies which of the following equations?

a) $a=b=c, \alpha=\beta=\Upsilon=90$ degree

b) $a \neq b=c, \alpha=\beta=\Upsilon=90$ degree

c) $a=b \neq c, \alpha=\beta=\Upsilon=90$ degree

d) $a=b=c, \alpha \neq \beta=\Upsilon=90$ degree

8. An Orthorhombic unit cell satisfies which of the following equations?
a) $a=b=c, \alpha=\beta=\Upsilon=90$ degree
b) $a\neq b\neq c, \alpha=\beta=\Upsilon=90$ degree
c) $a=b\neq c, \alpha=\beta=\Upsilon=90$ degree
d) $a=b=c, \alpha\neq\beta=\Upsilon=90$ degree
9. A Rhombohedra unit cell satisfies which of the following equations?
a) $a=b=c, \alpha=\beta=\Upsilon=90$ degree
b) $a\neq b=c, \alpha=\beta=\Upsilon=90$ degree
c) $a=b\neq c, \alpha=\beta=\Upsilon=90$ degree
d) $a=b=c, \alpha=\beta=\Upsilon\neq 90$ degree
10. A Hexagonal unit cell satisfies which of the following equations?
a) $a=b\neq c, \alpha=\beta=90$ degree, $\Upsilon=120$ degree
b) $a\neq b=c, \alpha=\beta=\Upsilon=90$ degree
c) $a=b\neq c, \alpha=\beta=\Upsilon=90$ degree
d) $a=b=c, \alpha\neq\beta=\Upsilon=90$ degree
11. A Monoclinic unit cell satisfies which of the following equations?
a) $a=b=c, \alpha=\beta=90$ degree $\neq \Upsilon$
b) $a\neq b=c, \alpha=\beta=\Upsilon=90$ degree
c) $a\neq b\neq c, \alpha=\beta=90$ degree $\neq \Upsilon$
d) $a=b=c, \alpha\neq\beta=\Upsilon=90$ degree
12. A Triclinic unit cell satisfies which of the following equations?
a) $a=b=c, \alpha=\beta=\Upsilon=90$ degree
b) $a\neq b=c, \alpha=\beta=\Upsilon=90$ degree
c) $a\neq b\neq c, \alpha\neq\beta\neq\Upsilon\neq 90$ degree
d) $a=b=c, \alpha\neq\beta=\Upsilon=90$ degree
13. Coordination number of simple cubic unit cell is equal to
a) 4
b) 6
c) 8
d) 2
14. Coordination number of face centered cubic unit cell is equal to
a) 4
b) 6
c) 8
d) 12
15. Coordination number of body centered cubic unit cell is equal to
a) 4

b) 6

c) 8

d) 2

16. Effective number of an atom in simple cubic unit cell is equal to

a) 4

b) 1

c) 8

d) 2

17. Effective number of an atom in face centered unit cell is equal to

a) 4

b) 1

c) 8

d) 2

18. Effective number of an atom in body centered cubic unit cell is equal to

a) 4

b) 1

c) 8

d) 2

19. Atomic Packing fraction in a percentage of simple cubic structure is given by

a) 74

b) 52

c) 68

d) 66

20. Atomic Packing fraction in a percentage of body centered structure is equal to

a) 74

b) 52

c) 68

d) 66

21. If radius of copper is 1.27 A°, then density of copper in Kg/m3 will be

a) 100.01

b) 86.25

c) 8979

d) 7968

22. Atomic Packing fraction in percentage of face centered cubic structure is equal to

a) 74
b) 52
c) 68
d) 66

Avionics MCQ for Aeronautical Engineering

1. Which of the following is true with respect to Head up display?

a) View and assimilate the flight data with his head up in a transparent display
b) Assimilate the flight data without looking at any kind of display panel
c) View and assimilate the flight data that is projected on the helmet
d) Using a head up display a pilot and view and assimilate the flight data in all 360°

2. Which one of the following flight parameters are not present in a typical commercial head up display?

a) Airspeed
b) Altitude
c) Heading
d) Throttle position

3. The main reason for using a collimated display in HUD is ________

a) More information can be displayed
b) Wide view of display
c) Information displayed is focused at infinity
d) Fast screen refresh rates

4. What are the sensors used in combination with a raster mode HUD?

a) GPS
b) LIDAR
c) Radar and FLIR (Forward Looking InfraRed)
d) Microwave radar

5. Which of the following is the correct order for the path of light in a HUD?

a) CRT -> mirror -> collimating lens -> combiner glass -> pilot
b) CRT -> collimating lens -> mirror -> combiner glass -> pilot
c) CRT -> mirror -> combiner glass -> collimating lens -> pilot
d) Collimating lens -> CRT -> mirror -> combiner glass -> pilot

6. What is the IFOV for a collimating lens of diameter 100mm, the distance between the collimating lens and combiner glass=50mm, the distance between pilot eyes and combiner glass=400mm?

a) 25.0°

b) 12.6°
c) 28.0°
d) 14.2°
7. Which of the following are not controlled by the HUD processor?
a) Power supply to HUD
b) Brightness level and contrast level
c) Symbol and font generation
d) Computing flight parameters
8. What is the contrast ratio of real world image to the CRT display image?
a) 1:1
b) 4:1
c) 7:3
d) 2:1
9. What is the reason for using CRT used instead of LCD or LED displays?
a) To meet the required brightness level
b) Cheap to manufacture
c) Low energy of operation
d) Lightweight
10. What are the four electromechanical devices retained while making an avionics update for old aircraft?
a) Vertical speed indicator, airspeed indicator, artificial horizon and heading indicator
b) Altimeter, airspeed indicator, artificial horizon and angle of attack indicator
c) Altimeter, airspeed indicator, turns coordinator and heading indicator
d) Altimeter, airspeed indicator, artificial horizon and heading indicator
11. OLED display is better than LED because _________
a) They are cheaper
b) They have high brightness
c) Do not require any illuminating source
d) Easy to manufacture
12. What are the 5 primary mechanical displays, a Primary Flight Display (PFD) can replace?
a) Altimeter, turn coordinator, vertical speed indicator, artificial horizon and heading/compass indicator

b) Altimeter, vertical speed indicator, artificial horizon, heading/compass indicator and Mach meter

c) Altimeter, vertical speed indicator, artificial horizon, heading/compass indicator and landing gear position

d) Altimeter, turn coordinator, artificial horizon, heading/compass indicator and Mach meter

13. Why are mechanical instruments retained when high tech LED displays are available?

a) LED displays are costly

b) LED Displays cannot withstand the flight environment conditions

c) Probability of failure

d) Accuracy

14. Which of the following is false with respect to multi-function LCD displays in cockpits?

a) High resolution

b) More information to be displayed

c) Bigger and customizable display

d) Take more space in cockpits

15. How many Primary Flight Displays are present in typical civil aircraft cockpit?

a) 1

b) 2

c) 4

d) 3

16. Which one of the following is false with respect to electromechanical instruments?

a) High cost

b) Require skilled labor for repair

c) Accurate measurements

d) Inevitable wear

17. What are the standby instruments that are combined in a Solid state integrated standby instrument?

a) Altimeter, vertical speed indicator, artificial horizon

b) Altimeter, airspeed indicator

c) Altimeter, airspeed indicator, artificial horizon

d) Altimeter, turn coordinator, artificial horizon, heading/compass indicator and Mach meter

18. What is the operating voltage of Solid-state integrated standby instrument?

a) 11V DC

b) 28V DC

c) 5V DC

d) 115V DC

19. Why is the BFW system used?

a) To control aerodynamically efficient but unstable body

b) For communications in aircraft

c) Better navigation

d) Reduced chances of enemy detection

20. How is fly by wire system implemented in an aircraft?

a) By using control rods and linkages connecting stick to control surfaces

b) By using high power radio transmitters and receivers

c) By using computers and actuators to control surfaces

d) Artificial intelligence

21. Which one of the following is not true with respect to the FBW system?

a) FBW is not necessary for every aircraft

b) FBW makes an aircraft stealthy

c) FBW provides better control and carefree flying

d) FBW makes aircraft with low stability fly smoothly

22. Which of the following is not a component of the FBW system?

a) Flight control computer

b) Aircraft motion sensor

c) Actuators

d) Communication receivers

23. How are FBW signals transmitted?

a) Simplex

b) Duplex

c) Time division multiplexing

d) Code division multiplexing

24. Which one of the following is a military standard data bus?

a) Mil Std 1553

b) ARINC 629

c) ARINC 429

d) COMAC C919

25. What type of cable is used in ARINC 629?

a) Coaxial cable
b) Screened twisted pair
c) Unscreened twisted pair
d) Parallel lines

26. Why are actuators used in FBW systems?
a) Movement of control surfaces
b) Reduce drag
c) Increase lift
d) Safety equipment

27. Why are both electrical and hydraulic systems are used in the same aircraft?
a) To generate more force
b) Quick deflections
c) As a fail safe
d) Hydraulics for more force and electric for quick deflections

28. The reason for using quadruplex actuation system is _______
a) precise movement
b) to counteract heavy air loads on the control surfaces
c) quick reaction to the control stick movement
d) as a fail safe mechanism

29. In a typical quadruplex actuator system, how is the failure of an actuator identified?
a) By comparing it with the signal of the three good ones
b) By comparing it with a simulation model
c) Using in-lane fault detection
d) Using reflectometry

30. Which of the following is not one of the functions performed by the FMS?
a) Automatic navigation and guidance including '4D' navigation
b) Management of aircraft systems
c) Efficient management of fuel
d) Housekeeping management

31. What does the outer loop of an autopilot do?
a) Generate commands to the inner flight control loop
b) Access the flight control surfaces to control the pitch and roll of the aircraft
c) Access the flight control surfaces to control the altitude and heading of the aircraft

d) Generate commands for the pilot to follow

32. Which of the following is the fundamental control of a common autopilot mode?

a) Altitude control

b) Pitch, roll and yaw control

c) Engine control

d) Automated landing

33. An altitude control loop does not depend on ________

a) Aircraft pitch angle

b) Angle of attack

c) Forward velocity

d) Density of air

34. What is the reason for choosing height error gain in such a way that the frequency of height loop is below the bandwidth of the pitch attitude loop?

a) Efficient flight

b) Better Range

c) Stable and damped response

d) Better climb rate

Thermodynamics for Aeronautical Engineering

2. A piston/cylinder with a cross-sectional area of 0.01 m^2 is resting on the stops. With an outside pressure of 100 kPa, what should be the water pressure to lift the piston?

a) 178kPa

b) 188kPa

c) 198kPa

d) 208kPa

3. A large exhaust fan in a lab room keeps the pressure inside at 10 cm water relative vacuum to the hallway? What is the net force acting on the door measuring 1.9 m by 1.1 m?

a) 2020 N

b) 2030 N

c) 2040 N

d) 2050 N

4. A 5 m long vertical tube having cross sectional area 200 cm^2 is placed in a water. It is filled with 15°C water, with the bottom closed and the top open to 100 kPa atmosphere. How much water is present in tube?

a) 99.9 kg

b) 109.9 kg
c) 89.9 kg
d) 79.9 kg

5. A 5 m long vertical tube having cross sectional area 200 cm2 is placed in a water. It is filled with 15°C water, with the bottom closed and the top open to 100 kPa atmosphere. What is the pressure at the bottom of tube ?
a) 119 kPa
b) 129 kPa
c) 139 kPa
d) 149 kPa

6. Find the pressure of water at 200°C and having specific volume of 1.5 m3/kg.
a) 0.9578 m3/kg
b) 0.8578 m3/kg
c) 0.7578 m3/kg
d) 0.6578 m3/kg

7. Find the pressure of water at 200°C and having specific volume of 1.5 m^3/kg.
a) 141.6 kPa
b) 111.6 kPa
c) 121.6 kPa
d) 161.6 kPa

8. A 5m^3 container is filled with 840 kg of granite (density is 2400 kg/m^3) and the rest of the volume is air (density is 1.15 kg/m^3). Find the mass of air present in the container.
a) 9.3475 kg
b) 8.3475 kg
c) 6.3475 kg
d) 5.3475 kg

9. A 100 m tall building receives superheated steam at 200 kPa at ground and leaves saturated vapour from the top at 125 kPa by losing 110 kJ/kg of heat. What should be the minimum inlet temperature at the ground of the building so that no steam will condense inside the pipe at steady state?
a) 363.54°C
b) 263.54°C
c) 163.54°C
d) none of the mentioned

10. The pressure gauge on an air tank shows 60 kPa when the diver is 8 m down in the ocean. At what depth will the gauge pressure be zero?

a) 34.118 m
b) 24.118 m
c) 14.118 m
d) none of the mentioned

11. A piston-cylinder device initially contains air at 150 kPa and 27°C. At this state, the volume is 400 litre. The mass of the piston is such that a 350 kPa pressure is required to move it. The air is now heated until its volume has doubled. Determine the final temperature.

a) 1400 K
b) 400 K
c) 500 K
d) 1500 K

12. A piston-cylinder device initially contains air at 150 kPa and 27°C. At this state, the volume is 400 litre. The mass of the piston is such that a 350 kPa pressure is required to move it. The air is now heated until its volume has doubled. Determine work done by the air.

a) 120 kJ
b) 130 kJ
c) 100 kJ
d) 140 kJ

13. Find the change in u for carbon dioxide between 600 K and 1200 K for a constant Cv0 value.

a) 291.8 kJ/kg
b) 391.8 kJ/kg
c) 491.8 kJ/kg
d) 591.8 kJ/kg

14. Calculate the change in enthalpy of carbon dioxide from 30 to 1500°C at 100 kPa at constant specific heat.

a) 2237.7 kJ/kg
b) 1637.7 kJ/kg
c) 1237.7 kJ/kg
d) 2337.7 kJ/kg

15. A sealed rigid vessel has volume of 1 m3 and contains 2 kg of water at 100°C. The vessel is now heated. If a safety pressure valve is installed, at what pressure should the valve be set to have a maximum temperature of 200°C ?

a) 431.3 kPa
b) 531.3 kPa
c) 631.3 kPa
d) 731.3 kPa

16. A system undergoing change in state from A to B along path 'X' receives 100 J heat and does 40 J work. It returns to state A from B along path 'Y' with work input of 30 J. Calculate the heat transfer involved along the path 'Y'.
a) – 60 J
b) 60 J
c) – 90 J
d) 90 J

17. Which of the following were used as fixed points before 1954?
a) The ice point
b) The steam point
c) All of the mentioned
d) None of the mentioned

18. What is the standard fixed point of thermometry?
a) The ice point
b) The steam point
c) The triple point of water
d) None of the mentioned

19. All gases and vapours approach ideal gas behaviour at?
a) High pressure and high density
b) Low pressure and low density
c) High pressure and low density
d) Low pressure and high density

20. The value of ratio of the steam point temperature to the ice point temperature is?
a) 1.466
b) 1.266
c) 1.166
d) 1.366

21. Celsius temperature of the triple point of water is (in degree Celsius)?
a) -0.00
b) 0.00
c) 0.01

d) None of the mentioned

22. Which of the following is chosen as the standard thermometric substance?

a) Gas

b) Liquid

c) Solid

d) All of the mentioned

23. A real gas behaves as an ideal gas when?

a) Temperature approaches zero

b) Pressure approaches zero

c) Both temperature and pressure approaches zero

d) None of the mentioned

24. The temperature interval from the oxygen point to the gold point is divided into how many parts?

a) 2

b) 3

c) 4

d) 1

Machine Dynamics for Aeronautical Engineering

1. A disc is spinning with an angular velocity ? rad/s about the axis of spin. The couple applied to the disc causing precession will be

a) 1/2Iω2

b) Iω2

c) 1/2 Iω ωp

d) Iω ωp

2. A disc spinning on its axis at 20 rad/s will undergo precession when a torque 100 N-m is applied about an axis normal to it at an angular speed, if mass moment of inertia of the disc is the 1 kg-m2

a) 2 rad/s

b) 5 rad/s

c) 10 rad/s

d) 20 rad/s

3. The engine of an aeroplane rotates in clockwise direction when seen from the tail end and the aeroplane takes a turn to the left. The effect of the gyroscopic couple on the aeroplane will be

a) to raise the nose and dip the tail

b) to dip the nose and raise the tail

c) to raise the nose and tail

d) to dip the nose and tail

4. The air screw of an aeroplane is rotating clockwise when looking from the front. If it makes a left turn, the gyroscopic effect will

a) tend to depress the nose and raise the tail

b) tend to raise the nose and depress the tail

c) tilt the aeroplane

d) none of the mentioned

5. The rotor of a ship rotates in clockwise direction when viewed from the stern and the ship takes a left turn. The effect of the gyroscopic couple acting on it will be

a) to raise the bow and stern

b) to lower the bow and stern

c) to raise the bow and lower the stern

d) to lower the bow and raise the stern

6. When the pitching of a ship is upward, the effect of gyroscopic couple acting on it will be

a) to move the ship towards port side

b) to move the ship towards star-board

c) to raise the bow and lower the stern

d) to raise the stern and lower the bow

7. In an automobile, if the vehicle makes a left turn, the gyroscopic torque

a) increases the forces on the outer wheels

b) decreases the forces on the outer wheels

c) does not affect the forces on the outer wheels

d) none of the mentioned

8. A motor car moving at a certain speed takes a left turn in a curved path. If the engine rotates in the same direction as that of wheels, then due to the centrifugal forces

a) the reaction on the inner wheels increases and on the outer wheels decreases

b) the reaction on the outer wheels increases and on the inner wheels decreases

c) the reaction on the front wheels increases and on the rear wheels decreases

d) the reaction on the rear wheels increases and on the front wheels decreases

9. A uniform disc of diameter 300 mm and of mass 5 kg is mounted on one end of an arm of length 600 mm. The other end of the arm is free to rotate in a universal bearing. If the disc rotates about the arm with a speed of 300 r.p.m. clockwise, looking from the front, with what speed will it precess about the vertical axis?

a) 14.7 rad/s
b) 15.7 rad/s
c) 16.7 rad/s
d) 17.7 rad/s

10. An aeroplane makes a complete half circle of 50 metres radius, towards left, when flying at 200 km per hr. The rotary engine and the propeller of the plane has a mass of 400 kg and a radius of gyration of 0.3 m. The engine rotates at 2400 r.p.m. clockwise when viewed from the rear. Find the gyroscopic couple on the aircraft.

a) 10.046 kN-m
b) 11.046 kN-m
c) 12.046 kN-m
d) 13.046 kN-m

11. The turbine rotor of a ship has a mass of 8 tonnes and a radius of gyration 0.6 m. It rotates at 1800 r.p.m. clockwise, when looking from the stern. Determine the gyroscopic couple, if the ship travels at 100 km/hr and steer to the left in a curve of 75 m radius.

a) 100.866 kN-m
b) 200.866 kN-m
c) 300.866 kN-m
d) 400.866 kN-m

12. The heavy turbine rotor of a sea vessel rotates at 1500 r.p.m. clockwise looking from the stern, its mass being 750 kg. The vessel pitches with an angular velocity of 1 rad/s. Determine the gyroscopic couple transmitted to the hull when bow is rising, if the radius of gyration for the rotor is 250 mm.

a) 4.364 kN-m
b) 5.364 kN-m
c) 6.364 kN-m
d) 7.364 kN-m

13. The turbine rotor of a ship has a mass of 3500 kg. It has a radius of gyration of 0.45 m and a speed of 3000 r.p.m. clockwise when looking from stern. Determine the gyroscopic couple upon the ship when the ship

is steering to the left on a curve of 100 m radius at a speed of 36 km/h.

a) 11.27 kN-m

b) 22.27 kN-m

c) 33.27 kN-m

d) 44.27 kN-m

14. The turbine rotor of a ship has a mass of 3500 kg. It has a radius of gyration of 0.45 m and a speed of 3000 r.p.m. clockwise when looking from stern. Determine the gyroscopic couple upon the ship when the ship is pitching in a simple harmonic motion, the bow falling with its maximum velocity. The period of pitching is 40 seconds and the total angular displacement between the two extreme positions of pitching is 12 degrees.

a) 3.675 kN-m

b) 4.675 kN-m

c) 5.675 kN-m

d) 6.675 kN-m

15. The mass of the turbine rotor of a ship is 20 tonnes and has a radius of gyration of 0.60 m. Its speed is 2000 r.p.m. The ship pitches 6° above and 6° below the horizontal position. A complete oscillation takes 30 seconds and the motion is simple harmonic. Determine Maximum gyroscopic couple.

a) 11.185 kN-m

b) 22.185 kN-m

c) 33.185 kN-m

d) 44.185 kN-m

16. The mass of the turbine rotor of a ship is 20 tonnes and has a radius of gyration of 0.60 m. Its speed is 2000 r.p.m. The ship pitches 6° above and 6° below the horizontal position. A complete oscillation takes 30 seconds and the motion is simple harmonic. Determine Maximum angular acceleration of the ship during pitching.

a) 0.0016 rad/s2

b) 0.0026 rad/s2

c) 0.0036 rad/s2

d) 0.0046 rad/s2

17. A ship propelled by a turbine rotor which has a mass of 5 tonnes and a speed of 2100 r.p.m. The rotor has a radius of gyration of 0.5 m and rotates in a clockwise direction when viewed from the stern. Find the gyroscopic effect when the ship sails at a speed of 30 km/h and steers to the left in a curve having 60 m radius.

a) 38.5 kN-m
b) 48.5 kN-m
c) 58.5 kN-m
d) 68.5 kN-m

18. A ship propelled by a turbine rotor which has a mass of 5 tonnes and a speed of 2100 r.p.m. The rotor has a radius of gyration of 0.5 m and rotates in a clockwise direction when viewed from the stern. Find the gyroscopic effect when the ship pitches 6 degree above and 6 degree below the horizontal position. The bow is descending with its maximum velocity. The motion due to pitching is simple harmonic and the periodic time is 20 seconds.

a) 6075 N-m
b) 7075 N-m
c) 8075 N-m
d) 9075 N-m

Machine Kinematics in Aeronautical Engineering

1. The unit of linear acceleration is

a) kg-m
b) m/s
c) m/s2
d) rad/s2

2. The angular velocity (in rad/s) of a body rotating at N r.p.m. is

a) π N/60
b) 2 π N/60
c) π N/120
d) π N/180

3. The linear velocity of a body rotating at ω rad/s along a circular path of radius r is given by

a) ω.r
b) ω/r
c) ωs2.r
d) ωs2/r

4. When a particle moves along a straight path, then the particle has

a) tangential acceleration only
b) centripetal acceleration only
c) both tangential and centripetal acceleration
d) none of the mentioned

5. When a particle moves with a uniform velocity along a circular path, then the particle has

a) tangential acceleration only
b) centripetal acceleration only
c) both tangential and centripetal acceleration
d) none of the mentioned

6. When the motion of a body is confined to only one plane, the motion is said to be

a) plane motion
b) rectilinear motion
c) curvilinear Motion
d) none of the mentioned

7. ________________ is the simplest type of motion and is along a straight line path.

a) plane motion
b) rectilinear motion
c) curvilinear Motion
d) none of the mentioned

8. __________________ is the motion along a curved path.

a) plane motion
b) rectilinear motion
c) curvilinear Motion
d) none of the mentioned

9. Displacement of a body is a ____________ quantity.

a) scalar
b) vector
c) scalar and vector
d) none of the mentioned

10. A train covers 60 miles between 2 p.m. and 4 p.m. How fast was it going at 3 p.m.?

a) 60 mph
b) 30 mph
c) 40 mph
d) 50 mph

11. The force which acts along the radius of a circle and directed ______________ the centre of the circle is known as centripetal force.

a) away from
b) towards

c) at the
d) none of the mentioned
12. The unit of mass moment of inertia in S.I. units is
a) m4
b) kgf-m-s2
c) kg-m2
d) N-m
13. Joule is a unit of
a) force
b) work
c) power
d) none of the mentioned
14. The energy possessed by a body, for doing work by virtue of its position, is called
a) potential energy
b) kinetic energy
c) electrical energy
d) chemical energy
15. When a body of mass moment of inertia I (about a given axis) is rotated about that axis with an angular velocity, then the kinetic energy of rotation is
a) 0.5 I.ω
b) I.ω
c) 0.5 I.ω2
d) I.ω2
16. The wheels of a moving car possess
a) potential energy only
b) kinetic energy of translation only
c) kinetic energy of rotation only
d) kinetic energy of translation and rotation both.
17. The bodies which rebound after impact are called
a) inelastic bodies
b) elastic bodies
c) solid bodies
d) none of the mentioned
18. The coefficient of restitution for inelastic bodies is
a) zero
b) between zero and one

c) one

d) more than one

19. Which of the following statement is correct ?

a) The kinetic energy of a body during impact remains constant.

b) The kinetic energy of a body before impact is equal to the kinetic energy of a body after impact.

c) The kinetic energy of a body before impact is less than the kinetic energy of a body after impact.

d) The kinetic energy of a body before impact is more than the kinetic energy of a body after impact.

20. A body of mass m moving with a constant velocity v strikes another body of same mass m moving with same velocity but in opposite direction. The common velocity of both the bodies after collision is

a) v

b) 2 v

c) 4 v

d) 8 v

www.ingramcontent.com/pod-product-compliance
Ingram Content Group UK Ltd.
Pitfield, Milton Keynes, MK11 3LW, UK
UKHW021913190726
13853UKWH00002B/655